Heroes Publishing

STAR-SPANGLED VILLANS

Steve Pennell

First published in Great Britain in 2007 by
Heroes Publishing.
P.O. Box 1703, Perry Barr,
Birmingham B42 1UZ.

ISBN 0-9543884-6-1

–

EAN 9780954388461

Cover photo: Steve Beauchampe

Printed by printondemand-worldwide.com

In loving memory of my Mom and Dad,
also Dave Nolan and Martin Dawson;
may you all rest in peace.

Acknowledgements

Thanks to everyone who helped with this book, or who make matchdays a bit more enjoyable. Mac McColgan, Richard Lindow, Steve Whitehouse, Richard Osborne, Drummond Murdoch, Steve and Paul Turner, Kerri Pennell, Kevin Beecroft, Neil Perrins, Gibbo, Tony Baldwin, and my lad Kurtis Cassin for his impressive computer skills, which helped a lot.

To Simon Page, Steve Beauchampe, the good people of the White Hart (including them that supports the other lot), and my colleagues at Chep UK, Marston Green – the hardest working men in Birmingham.

Richard 'Kong' Deakin and Vanessa 'Bubbles' Thacker for granting me the peace and quiet required to write again for the first time in five years. I hear Twycross is a nice area.

And special thanks to Aston Villa F.C. for being the greatest club in the history of football.

Contents

Introduction

I've just got back from the Villa. It was a nothing game against a nothing team – Sheffield United – who've done better than expected this season and thought they were safe. So we had a meaningless end-of-season stroll in the sunshine with nothing at stake bar a few hundred grand in prize money. The game was live on TV at a horrible kick-off time, with Villa comfortable in mid-table after a brief flirtation with the Premiership basement.

Yet there was a packed house, creating an atmosphere to rival any at the old ground for the last 25 years. After an emotional tribute to the 1982 European Champions, a scintillating performance of guile, power and pace by the current team sent the big crowd home in ecstasy. Some described the final goal in the 3-0 victory as 'Arsenalesque,' and the whole day was the best advert for next year's season tickets the club could have dreamed of.

As almost everyone present stayed behind to rapturously applaud the players on their customary lap of appreciation, it was hard to believe that this time last year fans were ready in their thousands to turn their backs on their beloved club. After a season of precious few highlights and even less transfer activity, the only talking points during the summer of 2006 were when would we be relegated and what players we would buy *"if only we had any money,"* which as an exercise in futility had little competition.

In truth, even chairman Doug Ellis had all but given up. He'd appointed merchant bankers Rothschild's to find a buyer for 'his' club, and even they didn't seem to be having much luck. One or two potential owners were reported to be sniffing around, but they were either a case of wishful thinking or the 'interesting' approach, no thanks, not even with a barge pole, of ex-Blue Ray Ranson.

As the same old players (minus possibly the best one, James Milner) reported back for training after the summer break, season ticket sales were plummeting and it was obvious to anyone with a passing interest in football that the biggest club in the Midlands were in crisis. For many of us who love Aston Villa it was heartbreaking. And yet things were about to change for the better in almost every way.

Chapter 1

The show begins

14th July 2006

The news breaks, via Sky Sports, that there's unrest in the camp. To this day their names are unknown, but it's generally agreed that 'some' senior players, having enlisted the help of Tim Nash of the *Express & Star*, issue a statement criticising Doug for lack of ambition and the total lack of money available to invest. No real surprise there, but coming from the players it's a bit of a shock. Footballers thinking about more than their wage packets and the price of Bentleys? Whatever next?

They made a few pointed remarks about having to pay for their own masseur and how Bodymoor Heath isn't being watered properly. All dramatic stuff, but what effect it'll have remains to be seen.

16th July

For the next few days Villa are regularly in the news, just like a proper big club, with claims and counter-claims whizzing back and forth between players, officials and angry supporters. There's a war of words between the West Midlands' two main newspapers, the *Birmingham Mail* and the *Express & Star*, over the validity and origins of the statement.

Pete Colley's reporting from Bodymoor every time I switch on *Sky Sports News*. He's on our screens more often than a new signing. Not that any player worth his salt would sign for this circus.

The club eventually hits back, wheeling out media spokesman

Phil Mepham to say Doug's fuming because none of the players or coaching staff had indicated they weren't happy and they're all denying they'd made such a statement. It wasn't very convincing. The players were hardly likely to say, "*Yeah, we think you're an old twat*" to the man who pays their wages, are they?

By attempting to question only the source of the statement, the club are admitting that the content may be true. They have an ally in the shape of *Mail* reporter Bill Howell, who reckons manager David O'Leary was trying to find himself a way out of Villa Park without losing his contract pay-off. Surely not? To further complicate matters, Howell and O'Leary have been at war for weeks, after O'Leary accused Howell of trying to stir unrest and said, correctly, that Howell was an Albion fan and, wrongly, that he'd been banned from Villa Park by previous managers.

The *Mail* has been calling for both O'Leary and Ellis to go for most of the season, ever since the debacle of a League Cup defeat at Doncaster. "***Just go Doug, and, for God's sake, take O'Leary with you!***" was their front page comment. Not since 1968 had the club's board been so under fire.

Howell and the *Mail* are fooling nobody. If the statement doesn't exist there's no public denial or support for the manager from the players, and certainly no talk of legal action. The club, to make matters even more farcical, now announce they're holding an inquiry into the statement. A statement that, if you remember, a few days earlier they'd said didn't exist.

Tim Nash, who broke the story, explains how he got the scoop in the first place. An 'insider' (there's a lot of insiders at Villa Park now) invited him along to hear what the players had to say, and he was shocked at their outspoken criticism of the way the club was being run. It was Nash who had the idea of saying it was a joint statement, so as to protect those concerned, and he who defended their actions "*They were desperate to get it out in the open. I'm aware as well that there are players who had their problems with David O'Leary, but everything I was told that afternoon was directed to the very top of the club.*"

Tim Nash had got the biggest story of his career. David O'Leary was probably feeling pleased with himself. Supporters were wondering how bad it was going to get. And four thousand miles away the owner of an American Football club, a man otherwise completely unknown on this side of the Atlantic, was watching proceedings with a more interested eye than you might have expected.

17th July

There's a story in the papers that an American credit card billionaire, Randy Lerner, is interested in taking over the Villa. We've heard these stories before; we've had potential new owners from everywhere except Australia and the North Pole, which means that next in line will be either Kylie Minogue or Frostie the Snowman. What kind of a name is Randy Lerner anyway? He sounds more like a porn star than the saviour of the Villa. Jonathan Fear, mouthpiece of both the Shareholders Association and the Villa Fans Combined pressure group (who in reality are one and the same) is getting excited on Sky.

19th July

To say the club's in turmoil was the biggest understatement since a Manchester United-supporting friend, sorry, casual acquaintance, of mine described our new signing Paul McGrath as *"quite good"*, but an article in this morning's *Times* brightened my mood considerably. Full of talk of Villa's huge potential, it reads like a gushing testimonial designed to attract the attention of any bored billionaire looking to blow their fortune. Events later on cheer me up even more.

The investigation into the players' statement, now inevitably dubbed 'Bodymoorgate', has been swift. After a two-day probe, the inquiry team of Steve Stride, Steven Kind and David Owen was ready to summon David O'Leary to Villa Park to discuss their findings. Many supporters, me included, hoped that whatever had really happened, the boss would be implicated, as after three years of talking the Villa down and the opposition up, he was as popular as a spot on a supermodel.

Like a kid waiting for Christmas morning the waiting seemed to drag on for hours. Eventually O'Leary emerged but said nothing to the press before driving off. Moments later he was followed by Phil Mepham, who announced that although no connection had been found between the manager and the statement, both parties had agreed to an amicable parting of the ways. It was, as someone tactlessly pointed out, a throwback to the days of the West Midlands Serious Crime Squad – glance at the evidence then blame the Irishman.

I heard the news via Radio 5 Live at work, and spent the rest of the night shift grinning like Barry Austin on Pancake Day. My friend, bloke who sits next to me, and sometime-employer Dave Woodhall was interviewed and said that he'd been in a pub within thirty seconds of hearing the news. I don't know if it was true, although I know that if he was, someone else would have been buying.

But there's no hiding from the fact that the crisis continues. We've got disgruntled players who only just beat the drop and an owner looking to sell. What kind of desperate, unemployed excuse for a football manager would dare risk his reputation on an attempt to bring order to this chaos? Billy McNeill's retired hasn't he?

Please tell me he has.

21st July
Walsall (away)

With his ex-boss gone, the responsibility for rallying the mutinous troops for the regular pre-season friendly at Walsall has fallen to his trusted assistant Roy Aitken. He's only been back at work a few days following surgery after a cancer scare.

At last! I'm going to a match! I like the Bescot. It's homely enough in a new ground sort of way and Walsall fans pretend to have some rivalry with us but there's never a problem. We have the away end and the stands down the side (nobody knows the name of any of the stands at Walsall) are mixed so we can be a big club that takes grounds over. A comfortable 5-0 victory does his recovery no harm at all, and Aitken was fulsome in his praise of the players, saying they'd made him proud to be in charge. Like all assistants he's angling for the job himself, without a hope of getting it.

25th July
Hull City (away)
Another routine win, this time at the KC stadium, which must be the worst name for a football ground on earth. Even at this stage the team look like they want to play again, which seemed to suggest that for all their supposed criticism of Doug, they weren't too fond of ex-manager David O'Leary either. How good those words sound.

26th July
Five Live's Pat Murphy brings unwelcome news, namely that Randy Lerner has pulled out of talks with the board and is flying back home. It's a blow, but softened somewhat by the inevitable press release from Villa Fans Combined and the Shareholders Association. He, sorry, they, say Doug should step aside. Now there's a shock.

28th July
Michael Neville's back on the scene. Last time he came sniffing around he claimed to have some Irish property developers, the Comer brothers, supporting him. Now all he can say is, *"I feel I have the backing."* Hardly a statement that inspires confidence, particularly as he reckons he's a friend of Charlie Aitken, who's never heard of him.

Another round of rumour frenzy gets whipped up when Athol Still, Sven Goran Eriksson's agent, was filmed entering the North Stand reception area. There's a coincidence. Sven had

told that fake sheikh from the *News of the World* he'd bring in
David Beckham if he was offered the Villa job. Just a coincidence, Steve. A coincidence. Sven is not, never, ever, going to be
Villa manager. Neither is Carlton Palmer, so you can stop worrying about that one as well.

A more interesting character is High Court judge Nicholas
Padfield QC, the public face of a group of investors who call
themselves AV06. And the fourth prospective owner is Randy
Lerner, back in the frame after yet more top-secret talks.
Everyone has an opinion, and with the internet messageboards
going into overdrive everyone's making sure the world knows
theirs. Are the potential owners genuinely interested in taking
the club over and running it properly, for the benefit of all, or
are they asset-strippers planning on making a fast buck? Like it
or not, it's down to Doug now. I hope to God he makes the right
decision.

29th July
Wolves (away)
Villa are at Molineux in a testimonial for Steve Bull and I want
to see how our poor, undernourished players are bearing up.
Plus it might be my last chance to shout *"Ellis out"* and I don't
want to miss that.

So I phone Dave Woodhall (it's advisable to employ a local
guide when going to the Black Country), and we arrange to meet
at New Street and catch the next train out of civilisation. As we
head west and back... way back into the last century... Sherpa
Woodhall points out local sites of interest. My God, that was a
short conversation.

Once in Wolvo we head for the Great Western, a traditional
English boozer that sells the kind of murky-looking real ale
Dave loves. Regards music, I prefer the real stuff to manufac-
tured Pop Idol rubbish, but when it comes to beer, give me the
mass-produced sort that actually tastes nice every time.

Dave does the ordering – he's fluent in the strange local

dialect – and I do the paying, while he gives me the inside track on Nicholas Padfield QC, who has been in contact with the Supporters Trust and sounds singularly unimpressive. Will this all end in tears?

Wolves used to be a right evil place to visit, but there's not a problem today. In fact we hardly see anybody on the way to the ground and we even walk through the infamous subway without a second thought. There's a sizeable contingent of visiting supporters in the 13,000 crowd, plus a retired travel agent in the directors' box. Maybe it's my age, but I'm beginning to find something distasteful about the ritual abuse of an 82-year-old who's had five major operations in twelve months. Of course, when he was healthier I was all for it.

Wolves kick off with Bully up front and it's sad to see such a legend looking and acting like a pub player. He gets on the end of one cross, the sort he used to crash into the back of the net without thinking. This time he takes a swing, the ball hits his leg and flies away. A few seconds later he's substituted and everyone in the ground stands to acknowledge one of the last great clubmen. What would have happened if 'Stayvie' had signed for us on one of the many occasions we were reported to be about to buy him? You can only wonder.

At half-time I get the first real chance to talk to a few of the old faces I know. To a man they're very glad O'Leary has gone but worried about what the future might bring. Martin O'Neill's clear favourite for the job if he wants it, with Alan Curbishley a distant second. As for a new chairman, nobody's getting their hopes up too much. There's even a few "*Better the devil you know*" mutterings.

Villa stroll to victory, with the third goal a beauty. Gabby Agbonlahor sprints clear of the home defence, and after giving the 'keeper the eyes, he slots the ball into the opposite corner. A comfortable warm-up, a useful run-out, and in spite of everything it seems whoever takes over from Roy Aitken will have some decent raw material to work with.

On the way back to the railway station we walk past Wetherspoon's on the high street and no-one comes out to chase us. Perhaps that's why they're called friendlies.

Chapter 2

New world order

1st August

Lerner's back in town. Well, not exactly flying back, but his bid, worth £64 million, is on again. Speculation is now intense that Martin O'Neill has been offered the manager's job. *"There is no announcement planned concerning the appointment of a new manager,"* are the words of Steve Stride. The media are talking to any supporter they can get hold of, which means the same two faces are on rotation again. Fear repeats the line that Ellis has to go, while Woodhall's is a less diplomatic, *"Just sort it out."*

4th August

I'm writing to the Press Complaints Commission about the irresponsible behaviour of Fleet Street's finest over the manager's job. Unsubstantiated speculation has triggered a mental condition, previously dormant since childhood. This clinically recognized phenomenon is present in up to one in seven people; symptoms include shortness of breath, irregular heartbeat, sweating, nausea and an overall feeling of dread. I came down with all of them on reading reports linking Glenn Hoddle, Graeme Souness and Sven Goran Eriksson with the Villa job. Its medical name is coulrophobia - an irrational fear of clowns.

There's only one candidate for me but until this morning I never thought Martin O'Neill would come. He left Celtic to care for his seriously-ill wife Geraldine, then showed his willingness to return to football by applying for the England job. The wise men at the FA gave it to Steve 'Mr. Charisma' McClaren instead. Thanks lads.

The Blessed Martin is not so desperate that he'd take any old job – he turned down Newcastle and Middlesbrough – but something about the Villa appeals to him. News broke last night that his arrival is imminent but seeing is believing so I've decided to find out how it feels to be an unemployed Newcastle fan and turn up at the ground to watch a new arrival enter the car park. I arrive early afternoon to be told the great man is due at around 6pm. The Aston Hotel is packed, and buzzing with what the arrival of the Messiah signals for the future.

"Doug will stay now he's pulled this off," is one view.

"No, he's definitely going or Martin wouldn't have signed," is a more popular one.

One bloke reminds us of O'Neill's interest in serial killers. The possessor of a degree in law, he apparently attended every day of the Yorkshire Ripper trial.

"What's your point?" I ask.

"Well... we've got Tracey Andrews." Words fail me.

A few Magners later and it's the appointed hour, hundreds of fans gathered outside the North Stand when Martin, Steve Stride and Doug Ellis swing through the gates. Immediately their car is mobbed by back-slapping well-wishers, and thankfully Old Doug is ignored rather than abused.

There's a bit of controversy when Jonathan Fear tries to get into the press conference – but the odd press release doesn't make you Citizen Kane, so he's left standing outside with us mere mortals.

I'm cutting it fine now for work at 9 o'clock, so as they open the North Stand for Martin to meet the adoring masses I make my excuses and leave. I'm very drunk – a health and safety hazard in the workplace if ever there was one – and very, very happy.

5th August
Various places in Western Europe

With Roy Aitken convalescing and Martin O'Neill keeping merely a watching brief, goalkeeping coach Eric Steele takes charge for a match against Hannover 96 on our pre-season tour of Germany and Holland, sharing the dug-out with new coaches John Robertson and Steve Walford. The game is a scoreless stalemate but no matter, the revolution starts Tuesday.

8th August

Eric Steele's been in charge of the team on the pre-season tour but as Martin arrives he's off and so, presumably, is Roy Aitken. Good luck to Roy – he did a great job in the circumstances and showed more passion for the Villa in a fortnight than O'Leary showed in three years. The new era begins with a whimper as we lose 2-1 to Dutch side NEC. The result doesn't matter as these games are all about fitness, but that said Mark Delaney comes on for about three minutes before going off injured again. There's bad luck and then there's having more time off than Father Christmas.

11th August

The usual low-key Villa pre-season tour ends with a 2-2 draw against FC Groningen of Holland, with reports of a few Villa supporters attacked by locals who think it's still 1985. One of the world's most charismatic managers has just a few days to weave his magic on players who less than a month ago were so demoralised they went to the press about it (The Samaritans were engaged). Good job it's only Arsenal away next.

14th August

I like Mondays as much as the next man, as long as the next man is Bob Geldof. But this one's different – this one's the best Monday of all time. Over the last few weeks I'd tried to keep up with all the takeover news but after a while it got too frustrating, not to mention confusing, and I gave up. This morning that little yellow ticker at the bottom of the screen on *Sky Sports News* tells me that Aston Villa have made an announcement to the Stock Exchange (in modern football the Stock Exchange is always the first to know, whatever Tom Ross might say), that they have accepted Randy Lerner's £62.6 million offer for the club.

Various statements are read out:

Doug Ellis: "*I am sure that this transaction will be the beginning of a new chapter in Aston Villa's proud history.*"

Randy Lerner: "*It is my belief that Aston Villa can compete at the highest level within the Premiership and in Europe.*"

And we learn about our new chairman from US broadcaster Doug Dieken: "*He is really driven to provide a winner, not just a winning team but the winner.*" Randy, who allegedly had meetings with O'Neill before taking over, promises improvements to Villa Park, Bodymoor Heath and most pressingly with two weeks of transfer window still open, the squad. The other consortia are still in the background, muttering about bigger offers, but it looks like the waiting's almost over.

18th August

I know it's childish, but the night before the new season starts I'm always like a kid on Christmas Eve. I read every bit of team news, look at every second of TV coverage and I can't get to sleep for thinking about what the next nine months will bring. I should have grown out of it by now but I hope I never do.

19th August
Arsenal (away)

Magnificent new stadium or not, I was looking forward to starting the season at Arsenal away like a dental appointment when the fixtures came out. Last season's five goal defeat is still fresh in the memory and I'm not hoping for much more than avoiding embarrassment.

Travelling down on Chiltern (Virgin have, helpfully, picked a Saturday when Villa are in London to sweep some leaves off the line) brings back memories of when our Inter-City firm could have been contained on one of those carts with handles that went up and down along the tracks. This train's full and everyone's quietly confident. Some pub I can't remember the name of is rammed out, with a couple of Stars & Stripes flags showing how we're becoming a symbol of American cultural imperialism.

The Emirates is a mighty impressive place, even if the pies are dear and they got no cowin' Bovril. We play 4-3-3 with Luke Moore and Gabby Agbonlahor supporting Angel from the flanks, as well as doing their best to work back and help the full backs. This work ethic is evident throughout the side and is the first noticeable sign of the new manager's influence. Stan Collymore, who played under O'Neill at Leicester, said *"Every one of his players would run through walls for him."* Getting Stan to run at all is no mean feat.

The game is pretty even, though as you would expect Arsenal do most of the attacking, until from our solitary corner Mellberg wins the honour of being the first goal scorer at the Emirates. It's backs to the wall from now on, and the Arsenal onslaught leads to a late equaliser for the home side, after which we seem quite comfortable. Arsenal play some wonderful football, but apart from Henry you wonder where the goals are going to come from. I would guess it'll also take them a few months to feel at home in these palatial new surroundings. Highbury was all tightly-packed stands and you could almost reach out and touch the players. This is something different entirely – there's a feeling of space and grandeur you don't even get at Old Trafford, for all its size. A draw is more than we expected, and when the players and manager come over at the final whistle, their celebratory mood tells us it's more than they expected as well. We spoilt Arsenal's housewarming party but another few minutes and it would have been the equivalent of stubbing out fags on their nice new carpet.

I run, or walk quickly, back to the tube station but still get caught in a huge queue, thereby scuppering all thoughts of a quiet journey home. By the time I get back to Marylebone the train's heaving. I toy with the idea of having a few beers and getting a later one, but Chiltern take forever at night and 'Er Indoors (sorry, I always come over all Minder when I'm dahn in the Smoke), or Kerri as I call her when I start speaking English again, is expecting me back the same day as I left the house. I end up sharing a table with three of Castle Vale's finest, who regale the rest of us with tales of how nobody wanted to know on the tube. Indeed they didn't.

22nd August

Martin's first bit of transfer negotiating is a pretty shrewd deal as Kevin Phillips moves to the Hawthorns for something like £700,000. He scored a winner against Blues last season so I can't think of him in less than glowing terms, but Phillips never really did much for us and he was injured for too long. If we can bring some old veteran in for the rest for the season it'll be a good bit of business all round.

23rd August
Reading (home)

I always look forward to the first *Heroes & Villains* of the season – a chance to renew friendships with regular customers and hopefully enjoy the good weather, for a couple of weeks at least. Not tonight though; it's raining enough to make anyone called Noah build an ark as I set out, and I always imagined the sun would shine on Villa Park forever after Doug Ellis left. But it's stopped by the time I get to my sales pitch – Woodhall's made his usual pact with the Devil – so I spend a pleasant two hours earning myself a pittance and him a small fortune while debating the latest news with the regulars. The general opinion is that Randy's about to take over and provide some money, but not a fortune. There's one or two who reckon he'll be spending Abramovitch-sized amounts, but I doubt it. All agree, though, that Doug is finally on his way out and it's a good job too, even his most fervent supporters. *"He's done some good things but he's past it now,"* summed up the feelings of many..

I don't usually take my kids to the match, but for the first day of the new era I get the missus to drop them off near the ground. Unbeknown to us we take our seats in the Upper Witton Lane with Reading a goal up. Then Angel crashes home a penalty and I remark to my youngest that at 1-0 with Reading down to ten men the game's as good as won.

It's therefore a shock to see the correct score on the concourse TVs at half time. *"It says 1-1 dad."* *"Typical Ellis, he'll do anything to make us look bad now he's going. Ask the steward what the score is."* Confirmation comes from the man in the orange jacket.

The second half sees a header from Gareth Barry finally overcome our impressive opponents, who look in little danger of returning to the twenty thousand leagues under the sea where lesser teams play. Judging by the way they performed tonight, once they get used to the Premiership there will definitely be three teams worse than them. Or maybe Martin O'Neill hasn't provided an overnight miracle. Maybe we still are mediocre, although mediocrity will be a vast improvement over most of what we had to endure last season. Jlloyd Samuel seems to be club scapegoat again, with Aaron Hughes his able deputy. I don't mind Hughes, he's a trier even if he is limited, but Samuel's capable of better. I hoped Martin might be able to get something out of him, but not on the evidence of the first two games and being substituted for Peter Whittingham, who I thought had left months ago, doesn't bode well for his Villa Park future.

The crowd is announced as 37,329 – good in the circumstances. It's a holiday week, Reading aren't the biggest draw in football and surely no-one but the blindest of the anti-Doug brigade expected an immediate sell-out once he was on his way.

35,000-odd of us are happy enough with the result, but not so happy when it starts to lash down again on the way home. Two games, four points and Villa Park's open again for business.

24th August

The size of the first -team squad shrinks further as one of the strangest transfer sagas of all time comes to a conclusion. A couple of summers ago, David O'Leary spent months chasing after French midfielder Matthieu Berson. Naturally, after making all that fuss we assumed we'd signed the second Zidane but when we eventually bought him, O'Leary, with the motivational skills that were to become legendary, promptly said Berson wasn't that good anyway. He was left out of the team for the first half of the season, came in and did a job. Not brilliant, but he looked good enough, so O'Leary naturally dropped him, put Thomas Hitzlsperger in his place even though he was off at the end of the season, and Berson never got a sniff again. No, I could never work it out, either.

27th August
Newcastle (home)

A pleasantly warm Bank Holiday Sunday afternoon, with the game being shoved back a day because Newcastle were in Europe on Thursday. Obviously we must help all the other English clubs these days, otherwise they might get knocked out and where would Channel Five be if they couldn't show UEFA Cup ties from former Yugoslav republics in front of a crowd of six thousand? Walking down Witton Lane with fellow-seller Mac McColgan, who's sold *H&V* from the bus stop over the road from my pitch so long that he's in the Centro timetables, I asked what it would take to get him back with a season ticket in his hand instead of picking and choosing. "*It wasn't Ellis, nor O'Leary, nor the football. It's everything,*" was the response. I know what he means; football's completely different now to what it was when I first started going down but even so it's still the Villa. It's

still my club. That'll never change, no matter who's in charge –
I hope.

There's a standing ovation from all around, including Doug, as
Randy Lerner takes his seat in the directors' box, even though
as the game progresses he seems to prefer sitting on the steps.
I'm sure the stewards will soon knock that idea out of him; Villa
Park stewards are an institution and it would take a brave man
to cross one, billionaire or no. Randy seems happy with life so
far but the first stage of his revolution will surely be to move the
club on from "*competing with the likes of Charlton*" (copyright
David O'Leary), to putting it on a level playing field with Spurs,
Everton and today's opponents. It might take a couple of transfer windows, but nevertheless, this game could prove to be a
useful barometer of our early progress. It's my first time in my
proper seat in the North Stand, and looking around me I see no
great changes. Dave and Rich, another of his wage slaves, are
either side and just over the gangway are a couple of old blokes
including Ray Fairfax, the ex-Albion player and former Villa
ticket office manager. Just behind them are the seats usually
reserved for former players. Even under Doug ex-pros were
always given tickets for matches, which is great as we can
remind Chris Nicholl about his goal in the 1977 League Cup final
or tell Des Bremner how good he was, but I'm not sure if they
want to hear it a dozen times every match.

We used to sit in the Holte until we got fed up with the inani-
ty of the nasty little faces behind us with their nasty little opin-
ions. I can moan with the best of them but I want to enjoy myself
down the match. I don't want to hear our players being called
the Welsh twat, the Danish twat, the fat twat, the lanky twat......
all season. So we moved to the peace and tranquility of the North
Stand, which apart from being a lot cheaper is also the best view
in the ground if you like being behind the goal.

Two ex-Villa men line up against us and there are boos for
Nobby Solano and cheers for James Milner. No prizes for guess-
ing which one Villa fans would welcome back into our side and

funnily enough, young James plays like he might be glad of such a move himself. Milner's quality, and I can see him slotting into this team a treat.

Despite a stuttering start first half goals from Luke Moore and Juan Pablo Angel put Villa in command and we play much better after the break without adding to the score. A friend in the media tells me after the game that a Newcastle player, speaking off-the-record, described Villa's total commitment to the cause as 'frightening', a testament to the motivational powers of Martin O'Neill. Despite the warnings that he likes the ball hoofed, we've certainly seen some nice football so far. Agbonlahor looks a different player to the one who first broke into the team last season and Angel seems to relish the responsibility of having Gabby and Luke Moore to do his running.

As well as being my birthday, tomorrow is also a Bank Holiday, so there are no barriers to getting suitably relaxed in the Adventurers after the game. The convivial atmosphere is only disturbed when the Toon team bus is held up in traffic opposite the pub and someone, who shall remain nameless, can't resist the urge to run outside and share a bottle of Magners with the passengers, by throwing it at the coach. Luckily, their accuracy is on a par with that of those on the bus and the shot flies just over.

29th August

And the sun keeps on shining. First Michael Neville and then Nicholas Padfield withdraw their interest in the Villa, which means the way is clear for Randy to take over. There's already talk of him selling the naming rights to the ground. This of course leads to the closest thing you'll ever get to a conversation with a Blue:

"You should be ashamed, an English club owned by Americans."

"Why?"

"Cos America's shit."

"Where did that pair of Levis you're wearing come from? Why are you drinking Coke? And did you or did you not have a Big Mac at dinnertime?"

30th August

Our new owner doesn't take much time to make himself at home because we're already talking big money for players. Despite Doug saying we're skint there's £6.5 million found to sign Stilyan Petrov, one of Martin's old players at Celtic. There's also talk of signing James Milner, who would be a good move. He knows the set-up and surely anyone with any sense would prefer the Brave New World of Villa Park to the freak-show at Newcastle. There's also a story about South American stars Javier Mascherano and Carlos Tevez moving to West Ham on loan. This is interesting – even I've heard of them so they must be good and if they want to join West Ham there's something seriously fishy going on.

Chapter 3

Chelmsley Chelsea

1st September
We never did get James Milner, as his transfer was stopped by the Newcastle board at the last minute. We've also got one of the biggest irritations in modern football coming up – an international weekend. It's an annoyance at any time. Three games into the season after a good start, it's inexcusable. To pass the time of day I glance at the record of General Charles Krulak, Randy's right-hand man. He's former commandant of the US Marine Corps, served in Vietnam and Iraq (that'll go down well with the locals in Aston), won two Purple Hearts and I think I've taken part in my last sack the board demo.

6th September
Somewhere in inner-city Birmingham
I know I should get out more, but I can't help being amused by a story in the *Mail* tonight about a school in Bordesley Green, naturally named St Andrew's, where the kids are now wearing claret and blue uniforms. This has so enraged the parents (i.e. two of them) that they've contacted the *Mail*, who sent ace reporter Lisa 'Scoop' Smith to report back on this astonishing affront to the nearby institution which has done so much to make the area what it is today. If it were my kids I'd be more worried about declining education standards and school discipline, but it just goes to show that, once more, 'obsession' isn't just a knock-off perfume, it's a lifestyle choice.

10th September

West Ham (away)

Upton Park is a lot more hospitable than it was the last time I came here a few years back, and on reflection wearing a stab-proof vest is probably a mistake given the lovely weather for the time of year.

The place is packed and the home supporters give a big welcome to their new signings Carlos Tevez and Javier Mascherano, although they both start on the bench. I get talking to Andy Wainwright, statistical genius, about the night at White Hart Lane in 1978 when World Cup winners Osvaldo Ardiles and Ricardo Villa made their debuts for Spurs and we won 4-1. Andy can recite every statistic there is about Villa, football and music, but we won't be the only ones thinking about that night in 1978. English football supporters must be the greatest experts on their given subject in the world. It's not just the anoraks – anyone who supports a team will be able to reel off a host of facts and memories. Recalling every detail of a match from almost thirty years ago is routine. That's why our football is special and one of the reasons why Randy's so determined to buy our club. Right back from the early Victorian days, the story of Aston Villa is the story of English football and it'll take an American to remind the world of it.

With the 'Appy 'Ammers shamelessly wearing our colours, Petrov barely has time to work out who's who before we go ahead through Liam Ridgewell, continuing his excellent start to the season. We're all over them, Angel twice heads against the bar and we have a couple of efforts cleared off the line. Petrov produces as good a debut as any since Dion Dublin's, and is particularly unlucky not to score when he lobs the 'keeper only to see a defender get back and scramble it clear. He definitely looks a star of the future.

West Ham get a fluky equaliser and as we tire towards the end they gain momentum, with most of the danger to our goal coming from Milan Baros's ugly little brother, Tevez, who plays half an hour and looks impressive. Although I might have settled for a point before the game, all those chances we missed make it disappointing to draw.

Coming out of the ground you can immediately spot the difference between us old school Villa supporters and our younger lot. We're heads down, not making a sound and moving warily towards the tube. They've got their Villa shirts for the world to see and singing about shitting on Cockneys at the tops of their voices. They probably think we're a bunch of girly wusses and they might be right. West Ham put aside organised violence in favour of entrepreneurial activities many years ago and unless you're Spurs or Chelsea, Upton Park's a safe day out these days. But old habits die hard and I'm probably not the only one to give a subconscious sigh of relief as I wander through the ticket barrier at Euston. I'm now safe to think about what to do with the £54.70 Randy's kindly offered for my shares.

12th September
We've signed the old Celtic defender Didier Agathe on a short-term deal. Hardly a glamour signing although I suppose it's only natural that Martin wants a few reliable players he knows to help him through his early days in charge.

14th September
I think it was Mac McColgan who said one of the problems with getting to know people who work for the Villa is that you invariably end up defending them from supporters who think they're useless or jobsworths because of their job rather than how they do it. One such character is the Villa's head of security, John Handley. Some might see him as in charge of stopping supporters from standing up and enjoying themselves, but in reality he's a very nice, very funny man who always has time for us. Today he made the headlines in his own way, when the *Guardian* leaked his report of an incident last season when Manchester City's charming Joey Barton swore at a female Villa

steward. John stated that Barton, *"responded with all the grace that comes so naturally to him by calling her a __ slag"*.

You might think it would be hard to get a copy of the *Guardian* on Chelmsley, but in fact only the *Sport* sells more in Fags & Mags. Remember, we get a lot of social workers round here.

16th September
Watford (away)

On the telly again, this time a 5.15 away at Watford. This means getting up at a reasonable hour and Kelli is dropping me off at the International rather than having to jump a bus into town. Luckily the train's not too full so Dave and I while a pleasant hour talking tactics. I like the 4-3-3 Martin's been using to good effect while he's an old-style 4-4-2 man although as I remind him, he was always keen on playing with three at the back not so long ago. My, what a riveting conversation that must have been for anyone overhearing us.

Watford's a nondescript sort of place, with the station miles from both ground and town centre. There's a pub outside the station but even three hours before kick-off it's rammed so me and the Astonian Rupert Murdoch walk up the road to this place he reckons isn't far away. Over a main drag, second on the left and to mine, and I think his, surprise, there it is. A pint of murky brown fluid for him, something cold and drinkable for me. We're joined briefly by John Knibbs, who last missed a match circa the Ice Age, accompanied by his wife Pauline and their lad. John's one of the good guys, and together with a couple of their mates we get involved in one of those meandering pub chats that the people on half a dozen different tables join in at some point or another. We're still miles away from the ground but the walls are covered in Watford FC souvenirs. There's something strange that I can't put my finger on until I wonder which live match is on TV. *"Who's playing now?"* *"Everybody,"* comes the reply. *"It's half past three."* Television has a lot to answer for.

Watford has always been a decent sort of club. They opened

what was then their new stand when Luton were banning away fans. Elton came out on the pitch, turned to us and said *"Away supporters will always be welcomed here."* Back in the days when going away was a social crime, things like that meant a lot. Then they gave us Sir Graham Taylor, so all in all I like Watford and I was glad to see them get promoted. That away end's horrible though. Trying to go for a slash is a nightmare.

Legend has it Aston Villa's first game was against a rugby team called Aston Brook St. Mary's, first half rugby, second half football. Our latest contest is the same but the other way round. We dominate the opening period when the ball is on the deck, and despite playing the kind of slick football that is becoming a hallmark of the new Villa, we go in level because of a familiar failure to take our chances.

After the interval Watford become Wimbleford as they bombard our penalty area with long balls and long throw-ins, while we just long for their inevitable relegation. It wouldn't make a scrap of difference to the Hornets' tactics were the game being played on the allotments at the back of the ground. The fact that Tommy Sorenson is undisputed man of the match says it all about our second half performance, and for once 30 seconds at the end of *Match of the Day* will be all we deserve.

To say we were on the defensive is putting it mildly – there hasn't been such a backs-to-the-wall display since American soldiers were let loose on Britain's women in World War Two. We get away with a point and I'm a bit worried now. Watford are going down, no question, and we couldn't beat them. Still, we're twelve places above Arsenal in the table and this is the type of ground where we've struggled too often over the years. As I return to Birmingham to find my home in darkness and fiancée asleep, one question keeps nagging away: Why in the name of Paul McGrath do I pay a fortune to Sky Sports and PremPlus when I spend time and even more money going to the games? It must be for the camaraderie of Villa's brilliant travelling support, because it's certainly not for the sparkling football.

19th September

It's ironic how many things end with less of a bang than you'd expect. I remember Thatcher leaving Downing Street for the last time, not dragged out kicking and screaming with a crowd of thousands jeering in the background but driven away waving to a couple of dozen curious onlookers. A few years before that the inmates of Kingshurst Comp didn't march through the playground en masse and set fire to the headmaster's office as arranged, we simply stopped going. This morning I was having a quiet snooze and a fag at work when Wes, a fellow Villa supporter, said to me, "*Doug's resigned. It's just been on Five Live*" on his way to the toilets. I shrugged and thought I might as well get back to work. Doug's gone, the rest of the board, except Steve Stride, have gone with him and the best I could muster was half a raised eyebrow. I'd never expected Doug to resign except at gunpoint, but with one Stock Exchange statement he's off to his Safe Little Aston Home. Strange indeed are the ways of the world.

20th September

Scunthorpe (away)

Glanford Park, Scunthorpe. A throw-back to the days when men were men and players in alice bands would never have got past the club commissionaire. It's great to stand on terracing again even if it does remind me of Doncaster, not so great when the programmes are all gone and worse still when they run out of pies. There's only about five thousand here for God's sake, it doesn't take a miracle to feed us.

Thinking Scunthorpe was somewhere near Leeds we set out in the middle of the afternoon and got there so early the man hadn't arrived at the car park. I think we saved ourselves £3 (but it might have been half a florin or possibly two pigs and a sheaf of corn) and decided to have a bit of a walk around, finding ourselves in the queue for a chippy. One young urchin in front must have been sent out hunter-gathering for the tribe as he ordered up two chips with gravy, two chips and mushy peas and one chips with curry sauce and peas, plus a mini fish, chips and gravy for the Alpha Male. It's a shame such primitive conditions still exist in this day and age. Couldn't Bono do something about it?

Obviously I'm not the only one whose thoughts go back to recent cup disasters like Burnley, Doncaster and Sheffield United. Why else would Sky's cameras be here, were it not in hope and expectation of another upset? Despite some hairy moments when Tommy Sorenson plays like Bruce Grobbelar with a bet on, the professional attitude of the players means that another clanger won't be dropped and a brace from the re-born Juan Pablo Angel is just reward for his efforts, along with those of Liam Ridgewell, who doesn't put a foot wrong all night. I was no great fan of his last year, but this season he's starting to look the part.

There are a few nailbiting minutes after Scunny pull a goal back, but eventually it's a case of job done and we're in the hat for the third round. Fair play to Scunthorpe though, they raised their game and play better football than bloody Watford. It's not being wise after the event, but they're worth keeping an eye on for the fixed odds.

23rd September
Charlton (home)

I like Charlton. Apart from the fact that Paul Weller's brilliant drummer Steve White supports them, the rest of their fans seem like a nice bunch too (except Gary Bushell and Jim Davidson). An inoffensive little club who know their place and rarely challenge the established order, if you're ever in need of three easy points you'd gladly choose a home game against the Addicks. That is why one of the most cutting insults I've heard about the Villa was when a Man United fan described us as *"like Charlton but with a bigger ground"*.

The growing buzz around Villa Park is in evidence when we

sell out of fanzines half an hour before kick-off, in spite of this issue being re-printed twice. Seeing the team run out before the game is a rare treat for a fanzine seller – God bless you Randy. Our Lord and Master's words are not repeatable. He regards every supporter unable to part with £1.50 as a lost opportunity.

The game itself is best described as a comfortable success, built on the winning of virtually every fifty-fifty tackle and lit up by two stunning goals. For the opener Gabriel Agbonlahor volleys home a wonderful crossfield pass from the peerless Gareth Barry, and victory is assured when Luke Moore bursts on to a defence-splitting slide-rule pass from Angel and finishes with equal precision.

Steven Davis is another who must be on a personal mission to prove me wrong. Last season we seemed to spend most matches with me pointing out, correctly, that he goes missing too often when everyone else, wrongly, was regarding him as the new Gordon Cowans. This season he's learnt he has to get involved more and the simple idea is often the right one. I still don't think he'll ever be a regular in a team that's going to be as good as we will become, but he's showing what a better manager can bring out of every player.

The table's starting to look a bit more realistic, with Chelsea top, Manchester United third and us fourth. 100% home record maintained, a clean sheet, goals from two young Brummies (both of them Academy graduates) and the ice-cold cider flows freely in the Adventurers' beer garden as the sun sets over the tropical splendour of Aston. I could get used to this.

30th September
Chelsea (away)

Some of my Small Heath drinking buddies, anxious for our unbeaten run to end, have been positively salivating in anticipation of our visit to Stamford Bridge. Apparently, this is the 'real test', as if Arsenal away wasn't.

With my finances being squeezed by the twin pressures of

impending matrimony and the 'aving-a-laff-John price of Stamford Bridge away section tickets, I followed this game via the good offices of some unknown foreign cable channel and the Fordbridge Social, a charming tavern in the quaintly-named village of Chelmsley Wood, itself situated in the borough of Solihull no matter how many of its residents claim to be born and bred Brummies. Chelsea score early on, aided and abetted by their twelfth man Graham Poll turning the first of many blind eyes as Sorenson is fouled in a goalmouth scramble, which is the cue for the newly-formed Fordbridge Chelsea Supporters Club (motto "*keepri'on*") to leap about with unabashed glee. I suppose they don't go to the match because they can't get the tickets.

It takes us a good half hour to get going, then Petrov takes the game by the scruff of the neck, in turn lifting those around him. A spell of pressure culminates in another home-grown goal as Steven Davis picks out Ridgewell, who heads across the six-yard box for Gabby to score.

Sorenson copes well with Chelsea's attacks after the break, and we have a chance to win it when Angel is put through only for Makele to rugby-tackle him, but Poll and possibly the gridiron fans on the Villa board see nothing wrong with it. The ref's bias becomes even more obvious when he stops a Villa break so that Shevchenko can put his boots back on.

Even so, we nearly win at the death as Juan Pablo hits the side-netting when it seems easier to score. I don't think I'm being one-eyed when I say we would have deserved it. One or two grunts around me indicate that the recently-disbanded Fordbridge CSC admit it as well.

Much is made of the effects of Champions League games on the top sides, and the fact that Chelsea faded late in the game after getting back from Bulgaria in the early hours of Thursday morning. But they're all professional athletes presumably in prime condition. A few hours in the first-class compartment of a privately-hired jet two days earlier isn't going to affect them that much is it? We might hark back to the old days at the drop of a hat, but I sometimes wonder if modern players don't have excuses available a bit too readily.

Two of the three hardest games of the season gone and we're still unbeaten in sixth place. The Blessed Martin reckons there's no chance we can carry this on, but what does he know about football?

Chapter 4

Former owner

3rd October

My share money arrived today. Randy's very kindly paid £5.47 per share so I got a cheque for £54.70. Some years ago I bought the old shares for what was, unknowingly, a bargain price of £100 each. In fact, so much of a bargain were they that one of the sellers ended up ringing Ed Doolan on *Radio WM* saying I was a conman trying to trick little old ladies out of Villa shares. It wasn't true but it ended my grand dreams of owning the Villa. I ended up flogging most of the old shares when the club floated on the Stock Exchange in 1997 and I, or rather the woman I was living with at the time, did the house up with the money. This time I'll be lucky to buy a week's groceries, but I'm much happier than I was when I was, briefly, a City Slicker. This time my shares are going to a good home.

It's strange how you can make so many misjudgements. I used to think Chris Sutton was a clumsy, past-it carthorse best suited to Small Heath, only they got rid of him last season. Now I realise he's a vastly-experienced and highly-respected player who, I'm sure, has at least another six months at the top. I also appreciate that 33 is not that old really and I've thought so ever since Paul McGrath turned 33 and started playing even better, if that was possible. There's naturally a bit of grumbling that Martin's brought in a Small Heath cast-off free transfer and we should be going for better but that's not the point. Sutton isn't the best striker in the world but he's the best available.

10th October

Unavailable for the foreseeable future is Lee Hendrie, who I'd describe as the enfant terrible of Villa Park if I could spell it. Hendrie's off on loan to Stoke, which is an utter waste of such talent. Stories abound of Lee's behaviour off the field, he's guilty of having more money than sense when he was too young to cope with it. We all know he can be a bit, er, hot-headed during the match but, despite rumours that his true allegiance borders on the unnatural, he always seems to love playing for us and nobody shows such natural exuberance when they score. The Hendrie sprint towards the family section in the corner of the Trinity Road after he gets a goal at the North Stand is a thing of great beauty and often makes us wonder the attraction of whoever's in there. If I were to say that Barton's regulars Mark and Louise Fletcher used to sit just above there, Mrs F hasn't renewed this season and now Hendrie's off, I'd have said too much already.

14th October

Spurs (home)

For some reason, Spurs is always a big gate, and a good day for retailers of unofficial merchandise. A great day for the *Heroes & Villains* publishing empire, the proprietor nearly cries with joy when we tell him how many we've sold. He actually does cry when he pays us. I discover it's a full house when some bloke approaches me enquiring about spare tickets – "*I've tried every trick in the book to get one,*" he opines. Apart from buying one earlier in the week, obviously. I'm never amazed by how many people assume there will always be a ticket available just because they want one.

The sell-out is due in part to my mate Kitty crowbarring the armchair Villains out of the White Hart (another picturesque country tavern in downtown Chelmsley) by organising tickets for them, but he shouldn't have bothered as all they do is moan that it's boring and leave as soon as we go behind. Why do we always seem to save our worst performances for our biggest crowds?

With Luke Moore out injured it's back to 4-4-2 with Baros back for what must surely be his last chance. He hardly took it, wandering around looking lost and causing me to have flashbacks to the workrate and never-say-die attitude of David Ginola. Eventually even Martin got fed up with him and brought on Didier Agathe, who was obviously not match fit but still did more than Baros. In fact, it can be said the act of standing up and making it from bench to touchline represented a greater effort than that displayed by our 'star' foward. Our other sub, interestingly, was Patrik Berger, who replaced Davis for the last quarter of an hour and showed there might be a future for him after all.

Admittedly, it's a dull game until the 75th minute when Angel misses a penalty then immediately compounds his error by going up the other end and scoring an own goal. It's a blow but the new Villa are nothing if not resilient and I have the scar to prove it – a long scrage down my shin as I jump up celebrate Barry scoring the goal of the month for October to equalize and Rich pushes me into the seat in front. Getting a point's worth the pain even if the goal wasn't in the greater scheme of things much to get worked up about. After all, Stuart Downing of Middlesbrough and England does things like that every week, doesn't he?

In the Adventurers after there's a promotion going on for the soon to be released book *Villains* by urban legends Danny Brown and Paul Brittle. They hand out posters and stickers, which later that evening cover the White Hart including one right in the middle of the TV screen. Blues fans are walking round the pub with said stickers on their backs, blissfully ignorant (which doesn't make much change) of the fact that they've become walking adverts for a Villa hoolie-book. Despite having a higher proportion of Zulu top boys per square foot than just about any pub in Birmingham, they take it in the right spirit.

16th October

In what will probably be the last time I take any notice of a Stock Exchange announcement, Randy now has 90% of Villa shares and will be able to compulsorily buy up the rest. And that should bring an end to the most heart-warming story to emerge from Villa Park for many year. Now how about we concentrate on the football?

19th October
Waterstones, High St

Being a literary sort I spend a lot of time in Waterstone's, because they've got comfy chairs and you can read a book from cover to cover without anyone asking you to leave. Today I spend a lot of time in a lengthy queue waiting to buy a copy of Paul McGrath's autobiography *Back From the Brink.* I rehearse over and over in my head what I'm going to say, how I believe him to be more than just a magnificent footballer but also a positive role model for anyone who has to face difficulties in their life. When I finally get the meet the great man all I can utter is a strangled, star-struck, *"Er... can you sign it to Steve please?"* Looking at the rest of the queue I'm not the only one acting like a lovestruck teenager in such a presence.

21st October
Fulham (home)

My friend Carl, a Swedish Villa fan who lives in Italy, is over for the Fulham game. When he first came to Birmingham on business a couple of years ago he asked his guides to take him to look at St. Andrews. He was not impressed. They then took him to Villa Park and he's been claret and blue ever since.

We meet in the Barton's before standing in the rain for two hours prior to the visit of glamorous West Londoners Fulham. It's another buggered-about kick-off time, this one 5.15. Not a great way to spend your holidays and it doesn't get much better at the match. There are signs of fatigue affecting our notoriously small squad, only supplemented this season by Petrov plus out-of-contract signings Chris Sutton and Didier Agathe.

30,919 is a poor crowd whatever the circumstances, but those who haven't made the effort seem to be the lucky ones. The highlight of the game was the presentation on the pitch before the game of Paul McGrath, presumably over here as part of his book promotion tour. In an unconvincing display Gareth Barry, taking over spot-kick responsibility from Angel after last week's miss, puts us ahead but Maurice Voltz gets an equaliser just before half-time. After the break Didier Agathe comes on for Milan Baros, which yet again says everything about Baros. It gives us a bit more width but not a lot else and with fifteen minutes to go Chris Sutton replaces Juan Pablo Angel, getting a few boos from our less enlightened supporters on account of his previous club, and with much the same lack of success as the man he replaced. It all starts to fizzle out soon after and by the final whistle there are considerably more empty spaces in the ground than there were at kick-off. Much of the second half entertainment centered on the paper aeroplane contest in the Holte. As ever, competition was fierce but the winner came from block K5, a sterling effort that caught a passing thermal enabling it to float gracefully past the stand and well beyond the goalline. Much like our crosses.

Fulham were well-organised. Their only aim every season is to avoid relgation and their tactics are suited accordingly. I hope they do stay up because Craven Cottage is one of the best away games of the season but it's still a game we should win. We've only won one out of the last six, a point Alan Green is only too keen to make, but we're the only unbeaten team in England and at the start of the season we'd have settled for that from the first three months.

I have to make Carl's visit memorable somehow so after the game we stay out and four hours later end up at Club Sensations in Moseley. At about 2am Kerri and her friend Amy turn up, and after checking I've got nothing incriminating dancing naked on my lap, owner Andy Browne lets them in and gives them a bottle of pink champagne and a packet of fags each. Top man.

24th October.
Leicester City (away)

I left it too late to get tickets from both of our allocations so have to call in a favour from my old Chelmsley mate, Leicester manager Rob Kelly, and once again he turns up trumps.

As a Foxes player years ago he got us tickets for an evening kick-off at Filbert Street, and a sizeable Villa mob went into the home end. Rob was on the bench next to their then-manager Jock Wallace, who was outraged by the violence. Rob had to pretend to agree with him but afterwards he admitted that he was secretly loving it. This was probably because although all little Chelmsley boys want to be footballers, their parents train them as hooligans first so they've got a trade to fall back on if they don't make it.

Midweek and not too far away it's a straight there and back car trip with my mates Kitty and his brother. The journey to the outskirts of Leicester is easy enough but we then suffer from the usual problem of all new grounds – the enormous traffic jams. Maybe its something the planners have to build in: "*Okay, we'll let you build a new football ground but you have to make sure anybody who goes there gets seriously annoyed at least once every game.*" We crawl a mile in forty minutes, eventually parking in a convenient space with the aid of a slightly illegal disabled badge. My Socialist principles make me uneasy about this flagrant abuse of the system, but it's getting close to kick-off and if we haven't got to pay then the money isn't boosting a multinational's profits.

Filbert Street used to be one of the liveliest aways of the season. It was always a three-line whip for our hooligan contingent and their lads were good at the Liverpool trick of picking off stragglers, which made the stroll back to the station a bit of an adventure. Not only that, but my belief in the equality of man always takes a battering as soon as I arrive in the city of Leicester. I've never met anyone from here who didn't have a bit missing. In fact, you never meet anyone from Leicester anywhere except Leicestershire. Think about it – I bet you know someone from Derby and/or Nottingham, but Leicester? Maybe they import a cast of actors to walk round the city whenever there's a match on and the rest of the time it's deserted, like a Wild West town in a Holywood film lot.

There's reports that the police seem to have got into the retrospirit by meeting Villa supporters at the station and detaining them for hours. It's my first time at the Walker's Stadium and it's eerily familiar. Of course it is; I've been here before, at Derby, Bolton, Southampton and all the other flat-pack out of town monstrosities.

Tonight's game is the definitive English cup-tie, an electric atmosphere created by a packed house watching end-to-end football although their supporters don't give ex-manager Martin O'Neill the reception I thought he'd get. I know they didn't like it when we took Brian Little but they haven't gone all Coventry on us and decided we're their big enemies have they? We take the lead twice only to let in daft equalisers both times, then have a chance to win with a last minute penalty but Barry's effort is saved. Come on Gaz, I've got to be up for work at five in the morning.

We finally edge it through Gabby's deflected shot in extra-time and five thousand traveling fans (including Lee Hendrie, who celebrates as much as anyone) leave the ground singing *"We are unbeatable."*

We might have been clever parking where we did before the match, but when we were 50 yards away 45 minutes after the match had finished it didn't seem like the brightest idea of the year. I later heard that after canceling some trains and delaying others, so the non-football traveling public were in some cases two hours late, the train from Leicester pulled into New Street at the same time as one from Sheffield, where non-league outfit

Birmingham City had been playing. You have to wonder if they do it deliberately.

26th October
Villa Park (second home)

And the PR work continues. With it being half-term there's an open training session at Villa Park. I go down in the company of 3,000-odd others, most of whom are either children or parents with their offspring. Not wishing to be accused of anything that might mean me ending up with broken windows I concentrate double hard on what the players are doing, and the results are surprising.

First, they're incredibly fit. I know they have to be, being professional sportsmen, but some of the fitness work they do, they manage without breaking sweat when I'd be unconscious within seconds, and I like to think I'm not exactly out of condition myself. As a result of that they're very, very quick. I can think back to when the likes of Tony Daley and Dalian Atkinson were the fastest players in the team but these lads would leave them for dead. Watching Gabby, he can't be far off the level of international athletes.

And finally, they're very good at what they do. Yes, it should be a given bearing in mind the money they make, but even players like Didier Agathe and Olof Mellberg are able to run up to a ball and hit it forty yards straight where they want it to go without a second thought. That might not sound too difficult, but try it yourself – if you're lucky you might achieve it once or twice out of ten attempts. These players can do it every time, without fail. It's all a bit unnerving, unnatural even, but at least expains why I'm in the stands and they aren't. And they're not the ones you think of who've got great ball skill. Juan Pablo Angel, meanwhile, is doing stuff that takes your breath away. Ball juggling, stepovers, the lot. It's an enlightening and, in more ways than one, worthwhile couple of hours.

28th October

Touchwood shopping centre (away)

Some weeks ago, Kerri took advantage of me by asking if I'd like to be really, really organised this year and do the Christmas shopping early. Naturally I agreed and so it was that I was sitting idly around the house while she decided which clothes to wear to go out and buy some more clothes, when I should have been on the train to Lime Street. Lunch at Café Rouge, Solihull, was a very poor substitute for the Arkles (even though it's full of Norwegian tourists and Villa supporters who think pubs are for anything but drinking in). And have you noticed these days that you don't get television shops in town centres? There was a time when every high street would have crowds looking at the scores in Radio Rentals' window on a Saturday afternoon, but I spent the first half completely ignorant of what was going on at Anfield, or for that matter what damage was being done to the Pennell family budget.

Eventually we decide to give the staff at Touchwood a rest and return to the car. I dive to turn the radio on to whatever BRMB's called these days and Tom informs me that we're three down. I switch off and Kerri wants to know why I don't want to listen to it after I'd made so much fuss to get back there in the first place. You can't argue with that sort of logic so I sit back and navigate to some other out of town retail park where she looks at other essential household gadgets such as radio-controlled eyebrow tweezers and biorhythmic MP3 players while I do the Man Thing and stay in the car. At five to five I can't take it any more and switch back on to hear that things improved slightly. Gabby showed we've got a very special talent on our hands with a goal that made the final score a bit more respectable and our second half performance bodes well for the future. That's one unbeaten run gone, now let's see how long the next one lasts.

Chapter 5

Running with the literati

After all the excitement of the last few weeks, this is the sort of mundane mid-table team you should beat with ease if you're going to be anything other than a mundane mid-table team. That's what pretty much happened as a penalty from Barry and a cool finish from Angel secure a very welcome three points. Tomas Sorenson's back after missing a couple of games and Chris Sutton makes his debut against the team he used to play for. It's only twelve years since he joined them for a record fee of £4.5 million and the rest of the world complained it wasn't fair because Blackburn were spending money nobody else could afford. Sometimes I feel like I was kidnapped by aliens one night and taken to a parallel universe.

Watching Angel score reminds me yet again of what a player he can still be on his day and how great he could have been. Dividing opinion like no other player I can recall, I've been mesmerised by his abilities ever since he signed for us at the end of what was a drawn-out transfer saga even by Villa standards, in January 2001. This was after the '£' sign protests, the *"Ellis - Spend Or Go"* posters that suddenly appeared on prime advertising sites all over the city and even a minor demonstration in the North Stand car park after one match. Angel's suffered from not having a regular partner and most of the managers he's played under have never worked out how to use him properly. He works well with Chris Sutton today, but that's never going to be a long-lasting relationship.

And a special mention goes to Martin Laursen, who after an almost uninterrupted two years out injured is at last starting to look like someone who might have once played for Milan.

While I love being able to watch the peerless Jeff Stelling on Soccer Saturday, the downside is it usually means we're playing on a Sunday. This seems to affect our attendances more than any other club, and the thirty thousand here today shows that despite the improvement in performances, the wider Villa public remains to be convinced that the years of decline under Doug Ellis are truly over.

Randy Lerner and his board have done as much as they possibly can outside of the transfer window, spending millions on renovating the Holte Hotel and planning the best training ground in the world. Yet it seems that cynical Villa fans, world-weary and sceptical after too many false dawns, will only be fully galvanised by a team that wins, and wins with style.

8th November
Chelsea (away)

And another thing Randy's done for us... laying on free travel for six thousand to tonight's League Cup tie at Chelsea. Me and Kitty are on coach 86 out of ninety-odd, next to old acquaintance and *Birmingham Mail* reporter Lisa Smith, and it takes a good half-hour searching Witton Lane to find it.

The whole exercise is described by some as a military operation but trust me, you wouldn't want the Villa Travel Club organizing the invasion of Iraq. Eventually we are on our way, and after whiling away the hours writing Lisa's copy for her as she looks after her daughter we arrive in West London. We also try to work out how long the convoy stretches and how long it will take to pass a certain place, based on a coach length of fifty feet, 30 yards between each one and an average speed of 60mph. Just as the coaches pull into Earl's Court Kitty settles on final figures of 14 miles and 26 hours. I reckoned it was nearer three furlongs and two days. These figures may not be accurate.

There's plenty of time for a pint before the game, and we sink a few in a swanky Earl's Court wine bar, where Brummie diners learn that the mushy peas they are thinking of ordering is, in fact, guacamole. London eh?

Standing in the Shed (never thought I'd write that twenty years ago), our high spirits are dampened when the announcer reads out the Chelsea team, which is probably the strongest Jose Mourinho could have picked. I was hoping they'd rest a few star names, but I honestly think that the prospect of Villa celebrating a victory in front of our magnificent support influences the Special One's selection. Kitty says if he'd known this in advance he wouldn't have bothered coming, and why didn't I let him know before he bought the tickets.

Martin O'Neill of course, apart from picking our strongest line-up, also picks our only line-up. Even so, I feel we're in with a chance until first Laursen then Barry go off injured within seconds of each other. This is a disaster that might have implications far beyond tonight. Laursen is playing superbly while Barry is in his best form for years. Our success has been built on teamwork – losing two of the team for any length of time could ruin the season.

They reorganise, Ridgwell and Berger coming on, but although they're decent enough replacements they aren't going to turn this situation round. Chasing the game, we give Chelsea the opportunity to pick us off on the break, which they grab with both hands. Another three times. The League Cup's always been special for us, and it's also our only chance of winning anything this season. Watching us making up the numbers on a night like tonight, which to be honest is all we have done, is worse than any Premiership defeat.

To make matters worse I'm also caught out three times – for smoking. Once in the concourse area, once in the toilet, and finally I'm threatened with ejection when an old dear in an air-conditioned executive box bubbles me to the stewards. God help me when it's banned at Villa Park next season. Meanwhile, our chav element is, well, in its element, swearing at stewards, smashing seats and behaving like I probably would have done if I'd had the chance when I was 14. There's nothing serious about what they're doing, apart from the bottle that got lashed at Frank Lampard, but it's all so boring. You've had a couple of pints and you know how to string two four-letter words together. Once is fine to prove you can, ninety minutes of it grates.

That apart, the rest of our support is wonderful. I know it's a bit Albionesque to boast how loud you are when you're getting twatted, but we all enjoyed ourselves. The result was an anti-climax but thanks anyway Randy, when I got home at two am I was still buzzing. It was a great day out and one I'll never forget.

11th November
Everton (away)

The city of Liverpool can, indeed, be a fine place. Music, fashion, football and the 2008 City of Culture. It's not really part of England, the contrasts between its public face and the seamy underbelly make it more like Madrid or Naples. I've had some great times at both grounds but I've also been frightened for my life more here than anywhere else. The League Cup semi-final in 1984, when the local bizzies looked the other way while pubs were getting wrecked and innocent supporters cut up remains the single worst night of violence I've ever known at a game. Now of course, we can look back on such times with fond nostalgia. The view from the away sections is poor and the facilities downstairs would give Lord Justice Taylor fond memories, but Goodison is one of the last proper football grounds and long may it remain so.

After a crushing defeat like the other night, accepted wisdom is that what's important is not the result but how you bounce back. But last year's performance at Goodison was so bad, easily the worst of the season, that it became the day Villa supporters, if not the chairman, realised O'Leary had to go.

Consequently I'm expecting us to bounce more like a dead cat than a rubber ball. It's a makeshift team, with Mellberg at right back and Chris Sutton starting his first game for us up front – which means, yet again, that Milan Baros is being reminded there isn't a great deal of time for him in Martin O'Neill's vision of the future.

Everton manager David Moyes has done a fine job in bringing together a crop of relative unknowns and making a team out of them, but magnificent displays from Ridgewell and Gary Cahill, Isiah Osbourne doing a fine impersonation of his hero Patrick Viera, and Gabby once again a potent threat, all go to show what an incredible academy we're blessed with.

Gordon Cowans and the rest of the coaches down at Bodymoor Heath seem to have found the happy knack of unearthing rough diamonds that, given the opportunity, can be a part of Villa's future for years to come. It would be churlish not to mention Doug Ellis's contribution to this. After all is said and done, he was very fond of saying *"I'd rather breed them than buy them"* and he backed this up by investing quite heavily in the youth set-up, obviously employing some very good coaches and scouts along the way.

Of course, you need the old hands to contribute too, and Chris Sutton carries the day with his first goal for Villa, a glancing header from a precise Osbourne cross. Keep it up Chris, and we'll gladly forget you played for anyone else.

We walk back to the car, pay the obliging youth two guineas for looking after it, he tugs his forelock and tells Kitty that he's a toff and no mistake, and make our weary way home. Normal behaviour for the journey home would, of course, be turning on 606 while footie fans around the country ring tell Alan about the appalling referee they've just watched, how video technology should be employed and which players should be in the England team. None of us have got a clue about any of that so we listen to a Ramsay Lewis compilation.

I get back to the White Hart in time to watch *Match of the Day* and when the league table comes on showing us third I turn to my Bluenosed mate and say, *"It's the future, get used to it."* He tells me to 'go away' or similar. Normal service is resumed.

19th November
Wigan Athletic (away)

I've been to Wigan a few times – the JJB, the old Springfield Road ground, the Casino for the legendary Northern Soul all-nighters – and Firenze it ain't. So today's game loses out to another event I've been looking forward to for weeks – the launch of *Villains*. There are so many hoolie books on the shelves nowadays that the club with the best firm in the country is probably the Writer's Guild, but an acquaintance with the authors means I have more than a passing interest in this particular volume.

I learned a couple of days ago that the planned launch party at Sensations has been scuppered by 'police advice'. A book launch stopped by the state – not quite Nazi Germany but we're getting there, and this is what I spent years screaming *"Maggie, Maggie, Maggie, Out! Out! Out!"* for. It's a real shame as the day promised to be a corker. The Wigan game on big screen, ex-players and celebrities, a charity auction and the real highlight – a bevy of dancing beauties.

All this was too much to re-organise at another venue, news of which was sent to me by text last night. When I get there this morning, though, plans have changed yet again. A couple of lads outside advise us of yet another location, asking us not to phone anyone with the details. I feel like a proper gangster.

All the subterfuge finally ends at the Roebuck in Erdington, where hundreds of literary aficionados are gathered, along with the authors themselves. I buy the book and get it signed by some of the main characters, then there's a general drift to the Swan to watch the match and I'm surprised to see a healthy away contingent behind the goal. Most of the faces that have become familiar to me from travelling over the years are in a pub 110 miles away having not left North Birmingham. I'd give a report of the match but in truth I only watched a couple of minutes, being preoccupied with what was going on around me. With so many vaguely-recognised faces from a dim and distant past, it was like a surreal version of *This Is Your Life* was being played out.

As the game finishes the silliness starts. First we're not allowed back into the Roebuck, then the police close down the next pub we're in, the Charlie Hall. It's a Wetherspoon's so they're used to lots of police turning up but this is probably the first time they've arrived unrequested. As the evening progresses West Midlands' finest flood the area, closing the pubs one by one. A few of us, finding it impossible to book a taxi, walk to the Yenton half a mile away and come across about twenty coppers in a side-street getting changed into full riot gear, all of this without a hint of trouble, because a group of people want to have a few drinks together. There hasn't been such an over-reaction since Rodney King got arrested.

The police are finally happy when they've closed every pub in Erdington High Street, but I can't imagine the local landlords are as pleased. The party re-convenes at O'Reilly's in Aston Cross, with a few hundred non-literary types drinking into the small hours, and wives and girlfriends drafted in to help the beleaguered bar staff.

I think Villa drew 0-0.

20th November

I didn't know who Richard FitzGerald was this morning, but now I know he's the former head of IMG's New Media International arm, as I believe the term goes, and new chief executive of what was Aston Villa plc and is now, hopefully, Aston Villa Football Club once more. In an ideal world he would remain in obscurity no matter how well he does, but this is modern football so he'll probably get as many headlines as Martin O'Neill.

It's all a bit of change from the old, infamous Villa board of Doug, his son, his lawyer and his doctor. It might take a while to get used to this idea of a non-plc acting like a corporation, but I'll try. Even pre-season is getting a makeover with, in what can hardly be classed as a surprise, Randy Lerner expressing a desire for Villa to visit the States in the summer. If he insists, but it'll have to go some to match the excitement generated by our traditional titanic tussles with rural Scandanavian pub teams. We'd better still play Walsall.

24th November

There seems to be a bit of trouble in our previously-happy camp as Patrik Berger gets shipped out to Stoke on loan, apparently after refusing to play for the reserves last night. The squad gets that bit smaller, but I don't think he'll be missed.

25th November
Middlesbrough (home)

If there's one team I can't abide outside the usual suspects (local rivals, the so-called big four, Leeds), it's today's opponents. The reasons are numerous, so I'll restrict myself to the top five.

1. George Boateng's misguided assertion that he could have become a Villa legend. George, listen... there's a real legend in the commentary box today. His name is Paul McGrath and if you ask nicely you might get his autograph. Don't ask if you can lace his boots though, you're not fit.

2. Steve McLaren's twisted view that Stewart Downing is better than Gareth Barry.

3. Southgate, Ehiogu and Boateng being unhappy at the stately home of football then ending up at that God-forsaken identik-it hell-hole The Riverside.

4. Their poaching of our backroom staff like Steve Harrison and Paul Barron, while showing absolutely no desire to tap-up our ex-chairman.

5. That fan who ran on to throw his season ticket at McLaren when we beat them last year. Like the Leicester supporter who attacked their keeper when we beat them 5-0, he'd seen them get beat nearly every week, but lose to the Villa and suddenly it's worth risking a life ban to protest.

Fair enough, 'Boro usually let us have three points at their ground by way of compensation, but be honest, their annual visit to Villa Park isn't one you immediately write in your diary when the fixtures come out is it? Unless it's so you don't forget to make other plans. Their away support always amounts to the kind of numbers we used to take to Norwich on a Wednesday night in January in the mid-eighties, so if they can't be bothered why should we?

Still, I've got a season ticket and I'm here anyway, so I might as well go in. It's another draw, comprising an offside goal for them and an unstoppable penalty from former England international Gareth Barry. Until we sign Kaka and Ronaldinho that's all the enthusiasm I can muster for a game against these non-entities. Baros comes on for Angel, and although he doesn't exactly get booed onto the pitch he hardly generates much in the way of support.

Full credit to the bloke behind me, Running Commentary Man, who as ever talks everyone through every incident. *"Go on Barry." "Angel got fouled there." "There's a shot on here." "That was offside."* I'm sure you know the sort. In the same way that presenters on shopping channels have to talk about mundane objects for half an hour to get a job, so he deserves praise for being able to find ninety minutesworth this afternoon.

29th November
Manchester City (home)

There might be something special about night matches when there's a big gate and an important occasion, but for a mundane league match with Manchester City it means catching the number eight because my chauffeur can't be bothered to pick me up from work, then standing around for a couple of hours in the dark while watching the traffic inch past on the Expressway. With fifteen minutes to go the crowds start to pick up and everyone's in a rush. It says a lot about modern football supporters and the influence of television that there's a big proportion of the crowd who assume it's an eight o'clock kick-off.

What is it about playing the Villa that turns Manchester City into such a good side, no matter how bad they are against everybody else? Whatever it is it's bloody annoying. Once more we watch mystified as Distin morphs into Franz Beckenbaur, Barton plays like a combination of Dennis Mortimer and Sid Cowans, and even Darius rediscovers the whereabouts of those white wooden frames at either end of the pitch. Next week mark my words, they'll all be rubbish again.

The greasy surface is perfect for City's slick passing game (I can't believe I just said that), and they're two up after 45 minutes when we hardly get the ball off them, never mind do anything with it. Gavin McCann, with the white streak in his hair making him look like a cross between Dickie Davis and Gomez Adams, fires in a beauty to raise our hopes of getting back into it, and for a while we apply some pressure on the City defence.

Then one of our attacks crumbles on the impregnable fortress that is Sylvain Distin and he plays a lovely one-two out of defence and runs the length of the pitch before finishing coolly. He is now doing Lothar Mattheus impressions. Another crowd that struggles to get over thirty thousand, even allowing for a good City turnout, and once more they're leaving in droves well before the final whistle. If Randy's here he must be starting to wonder if he should have stuck to armour-plated rugby.

A few weeks ago I was looking forward to this month more than most – with trips to Chelsea and Everton sandwiched between three winnable home games and Paul Weller at Wolverhampton Civic Hall on the 30th. The football's been crap so Paul, don't let me down tomorrow night.

30th November

Paul Weller is God.

Elsewhere, Doug Ellis gave a long and rambling interview with *Five Live* in which, amongst other things, he praised himself for appointing Martin O'Neill and promised to offer advice to Randy Lerner whenever it was needed. This time last year I'd have thrown things through the window at the sound of such arrogance but now I can even feel a bit of pity for the old fella. You can tell he really has nothing once he drives away from Villa Park at night.

Chapter 6

Presenting gifts

2nd December

Portsmouth (away)

The trip down here's one of my favourite away games now the 6.57 crew have (hopefully) retired. On the way down we talk about memorable trips to the south coast, most of which have ended in draws and getting soaked. It's one of those places you used to get to on endless journeys along A-roads where you'd stop half a dozen times to terrorise small villages and Little Chefs. Now it's a relatively painless three hours on the motorway and the 21st century equivalent of Little Chef are getting their own back by charging £43.95 for a 'Mega-Breakfast.'

I stayed in last night, so I'm bright-eyed and bushy-tailed for when Kitty arrives to transport me to the south. We get to Fratton for one and park up surprisingly close to the ground. A proper ground with floodlights (although still no roof on the away end), always a good atmosphere and usually a good game, and today's no exception. Villa's play improves immeasurably after the chasing we got Wednesday night and following a lightning break from Steve Davis and a foul on Gabby by ex-Villa keeper David James, we take the lead through new penalty king Gareth Barry. James is lucky not to be sent off, but the referee is Uriah Rennie and Scooby-Doo appears less confused than him most of the time.

Let's not forget that Pompey are pretty formidable at home so when they go 2-1 up thanks to a double from Matty Taylor and get that crowd behind them it looks like another defeat is on the cards. Then the much-maligned Juan Pablo comes off the bench to smash home his seventh goal of the season and earn us a valuable point.

Song of the day is a toss-up between *"Shall we ring a bell for you?"* to the Pompey fans, and *"You've got hair like me granddad"* to David James. Incidentally, can someone please explain why James, good servant though he was despite losing us the 2000 Cup Final, gets such a good reception from Villa fans, while Darius Vassell, who always has and always will be a supporter of the club, gets booed?

On the way back we had one of those amusing occurrences that remind you of days gone by. We were traveling up the A34 when one of our number suggested a stop off. We drive into a promising village and make for the nearest pub. It's about seven o'clock by now and as I wandered up to the bar the landlord chipped in with *"Been to the match lads?"* *"That's right,"* I replied. *"Just on our way home and we thought we'd nip in for a quick one."*

"Not here you don't. No football supporters allowed. Now get moving or I'll ring the police."

There was nowhere else in sight and we didn't fancy driving around only to get a repeat of the hostile hostelry so we got back on the road and ended up home earlier than anticipated. At a time when the whole country seems to be falling over itself to profess a love of football, it's good to be reminded that there are some whose attitudes are still rooted in the eighties. Long may such customer service continue.

11th December
Sheffield United (away)
It is, of course, a source of considerable amusement that this is the nearest away game of the season. An easy drive up, get parked and a few beers in a pub close to the ground. It's all you hope for at an away, until kick-off at least. And given last season's form it was all you could hope for including the match as

well. We end up talking to some of the locals who are so far gone by seven o'clock that they don't notice when we start competing with each other to see who can do the broadest fake Yorkshire accent. Drummond, fellow *H&V* seller and resident of some former pit village within walking distance, got disqualified when he asked the barmaid for a barm cake. Taking the piss is one thing but that was abusing the privilege.

Standing outside the ground I bump into Dennis Dudley, solicitor to the stars, and he reminds me about what happened last time we played a local derby on a Monday night, namely a defeat to Small Heath three years ago. There's a good crowd, helped by United's sensible pricing policy and the distribution of lots of free tickets to the local student population. Thinking about our regular special offers I wonder how often this goes on and how it inflates average crowds in the Greatest League in the World. Stan Petrov scores his first Villa goal after ninety seconds and it does him the world of good, elevating his performance from the ordinary of the last few games to the majesty of his debut back in September. It's another game we should kill off before halftime but a lack of quality in front of goal and a wrong offside decision when Gabby nets leaves t'Blairdes still in wi' a shout.

They come storming back into it after the break with Villa struggling to find any composure on the ball, but to our credit we don't allow this to affect our ability to give every last ounce of effort. No sooner do we find ourselves behind than we hit back with Milan Baros tieing the scores at 2-2 and that's how it finishes. There's a bit of an altercation after Juan Pablo Angel, who replaced Chris Sutton after 83 minutes when Sutton had clearly given his all and a bit more besides, elbows a Sheffield United player but it comes to nothing although we later heard that the teams were squaring up in the players' tunnel. How about that? We're turning into Arsenal. Sutton's reward for sweating blood was a standing ovation from all but the moron two rows in front who explained loudly that he's "*not clapping no Bluenose*". Such a shame that Care in the Community doesn't always work, and him being allowed to stay up after dark as well.

Like Pompey, it's another great spectacle for the neutral and should go a long way towards getting rid of the 'boring' reputation that's stuck to the Villa ever since the 2000 cup final. All these draws are becoming predictable but having said that, an away point is nearly always a decent result in the Premier League, the last exception I can think of being that Fulham game when Juan Pablo missed two penalties.

A comedy moment that I didn't really appreciate until I got home and watched the match on tape (yes, I know it's sad) occurred when a ball-boy slips over and makes a right pig's ear of returning the ball right in front of the Villa fans. We serenade him with *"You're getting sacked in the morning,"* he laughs as hard as anyone and approaches a Villa fan with his outstretched hand offered in friendship, only to get done by the old handshake trick. One for *Soccer AM* methinks. Not that I watch *Soccer AM*, of course. Oh no.

12th December

I know I keep saying just when you think it can't get any better it does, but I really didn't think it could get any better and it has. The Villa have announced plans for a redevelopment of the Holte Hotel that's been stood abandoned for years. It'll cost something like £4 million. I celebrate by popping into the White Hart and asking the first Bluenose I see, *"We're spending four million doing up a pub. How much do you think we'll spend on players?"* Half an hour later, after I've finished my drink, I look back to see him still counting on his fingers.

16th December
Bolton Wanderers (home)

Standing outside the ground peddling quality unofficial literature you can usually tell what the crowd's going to be like. When there's long periods with nobody walking past at all chances are there'll be a lot less than thirty thousand inside and that's what we get today, with a reported attendance of 27,450 and blocks of empty seats. There are also a lot of obvious gaps in the middle of the Trinity Road and Witton Lane stands which show that a number of season ticket holders haven't bothered to stir themselves a week before Christmas. I can sort-of see their point because Bolton are a horrible team who play horrible football, although we do have a new signing in the form of emergency loan star Gabor Kiraly, signed from Crystal Palace earlier in the week because Stuart Taylor and Tomas Sorenson are out injured. Further injuries mean that none of our wide players are in their proper positions. Our right side naturally play in the centre while our left-back is the best English midfield player on current form and in front of him is the country's most promising young striker. You can only get away with emergency measures like that for so long.

Kiraly wears very bad tracksuit bottoms but that's about all he has to do for above an hour as we play some decent football. Bolton's keeper Jussi Jaaskelainan – who Doug would have loved to sign purely for the cost of the letters on his shirt – is throwing himself around in a successful attempt to keep us from scoring. When things like this happen there's always one predictable outcome and it comes with sixteen minutes to go when Stilyan Petrov tangles with Nicholas Anelka inside our box. The resulting, inevitable, penalty is put away by the octogenarian Gary Speed and even the diehards who've turned up this afternoon begin to drift away. I spend the rest of the game wondering whether the cynics are right and we haven't got the potential support to fill a bigger ground. Granted, it's probably the least attractive opposition in the league but there was talk about how the ground would be full for every match in the Brave New World. That was never going to happen, but 27,450? At least there's a bit of a stir originating from one of the Trinity Road boxes, where a few scribes on their Christmas works do are adding to the festive air with some choice vintage terrace anthems.

We've played well and should have scored a couple but it's Bolton and their profoundly irritating manager who are now level on points with fourth-placed Arsenal and making noises about doing well for such a little team. There should be something praiseworthy about a club with no support and very little money matching the elite but this is Bolton and Sam Allardyce we're taking about. We're eighth, and the gap between us and Europe is already starting to grow.

23rd December
Manchester United (home)

Kitty gets caught cold by the early sell-out, so I tell him that if he comes to the Ads with me to watch the game on Al Jazeera his son Lee can have my ticket. These days, demand for the big games is huge yet we still get crowds like the one against Bolton. I suppose that's the joy of the Premier League, but the opposition mean less than nothing to me – I only come to see the Villa, so Manchester United and the inevitable defeat is my least-favourite game of the season.

My only regret is missing the return of Ron Saunders to Villa Park for the first time since Tony Barton's memorial match in 1994. There were only a couple of thousand at that game, with no sign of the multitudes who were later to be found baying for Doug's blood over his refusal to pay adequate tribute to the 1982 European champions. By all accounts Mr Saunders gets a warm, but hardly rapturous, reception. Those who know, know, but there are many Villa Park attenders who are only interested in the here and now. The *H&V* sellers stationed on Witton Lane and he often tells me about absolute legends, the likes of Dennis Mortimer and Peter McParland, walking towards the ground without being recognised by today's support. That's the 'Preeemier' League for you.

As usual with games at home to United, Villa hold their own quite well for about an hour but never look like there's a goal in any of our team. Then a mistake by Aaron Hughes, cementing his role as team scapegoat while Jlloyd Samuel's not playing, leads to a Ronaldo breakaway that ends with the first goal. There's no way back from this and United go on to add two more, including a Scholes volley so good we could see even on TV that it was applauded by Villa fans.

At least, I presume they were Villa fans, as one of the most annoying things about home games against Manchester United (and Liverpool), is the number of interlopers who jump up in the home areas when (not if) they score. This is not a problem one encounters at the Ads, where the doorman on matchdays is such a daunting character you have to have known him for at least ten years before you even dare ask if you can come into his pub.

At least the circus has left town for another year and I can get on with celebrating Christmas. I've asked for a Jam reunion gig at the rebuilt Wigan Casino. Last year I asked for a billionaire to take the Villa over so I'm on a winning streak.

26th December
Tottenham Hotspur (away)
A patched-up Villa side head to the capital without me, as a combination of yesterday's over indulgence and non-existent public transport means I'll be watching at home. When I say home I mean yet another pub with Arab satellite reception. Watching the Villa in such surroundings won't be so easy next year as I hear this channel has lost their Premier League contract and pubs will have to install new expensive two metre dishes to receive games not being shown on Sky and Setanta. I wonder how they can be disguised.

Sod's law is in full effect today as Jermain Defoe first passes a late fitness test, then scores twice to settle a contest in which Villa compete quite well, all things considered. Indeed, most people in the pub comment that Defoe's the difference between the two sides, although my own opinion is that Berbatov, who sets up both goals, is the kind of player we are missing. But in reality it goes much deeper than that.

Having a team on the pitch and another in the stands isn't a luxury reserved for Real Madrid and Milan anymore; it's the only way you're going to make an impression in the Premiership. We're doing well until both Mellberg and Hughes injure themselves and from then on the result is never really in doubt, even if we do make Spurs wait an hour for their opening goal. There's a mixed crowd in the pub but the season of good-will means nobody gets too upset even though my Christmas cheer was stretched almost to breaking point when somebody who I'd earlier overheard asking which one was Angel could be heard telling everyone in the pub how O'Neill was a useless Irish twat and we should get Terry Venables in.

You can point out that we finished the game with seven academy graduates on the pitch (average age 21), in front of a goalkeeper who can't get a game for Crystal Palace but what's the use? It's a nightmare vision of what might have been our future had Randy Lerner not rescued us from the dead hand of Doug on the tiller, not to mention his vice-like grip on the purse-strings. We still need some new players, and the transfer window can't open quick enough, but Christmas certainly came early for us this year, even if it didn't deliver me Bruce, Rick and Paul.

30th December
Charlton Athletic (away)

It's amazing how the mood surrounding Villa has changed since we beat Everton to go third in the league. Coming out of that game everyone was all smiles and confident that world domination would soon be ours, and I had a bet with the White Hart's resident bookie that we'd end the season with sixty points or more. Looking back the only one not fooled by our flying start was Martin O'Neill, which is why he's a football manager and I repair pallets.

The fates are truly conspiring against us at the moment, and just when we could do with playing a team with an incompetent buffoon like Les Reed in charge, Charlton sack him and appoint Alan Pardew. No Brian Clough, but regardless of the individual concerned, new manager syndrome is still one of the most powerful forces in football.

It's a 12.45 kick-off so up while it's still dark, talk Kerri into driving me to the International and on the ten o'clock to Euston. I can never understand what it is that possesses otherwise-normal young men to drink alcohol as soon as they enter a train. I didn't do it even when I was young and normal, but at least the sight of a four-pack of Stellas is a sign that the inhabitants of that table are best avoided.

Into Euston, onto the tube to London Bridge and the overland south of the river. Millwall's ground looks intimidating even when they're playing away and as the train pulls into Charlton station I wonder, not for the first time, how two teams in such close proximity can have supporters with such different attitudes. I should be used to it by now.

Charlton are a perfect example of how to run a smallish football club. They were perennial strugglers, even going into administration then having to sell their ground at one point but they kept plugging away, moved back to the Valley after a fans' campaign that was an inspiration to football supporters everywhere and managed to compete in the old first division on crowds a quarter of most. Like Wimbledon they were a pain to play against, but unlike Wimbledon they regrouped when they got relegated, used the top-heavy income available to their advantage and established themselves in the Premiership with decent gates and a tidy enough ground in a setting that isn't really London at all. They were always going to struggle without Alan Curbishley as manager, but they should still have enough quality to stay up.

We've sold out our allocation again, which is pretty good for a televised match on Christmas Saturday. Our all-conquering team of grizzled FA Youth Cup veterans starts well, and even go ahead through a penalty from Barry. Captain Marvel is without question our best player, in whatever position he plays, and you have to wonder where we'd be without him. You also have to wonder, or rather worry, if he's starting to think where he'd be without us.

We're soon to find out, as after Charlton equalise, he's sent off for a professional foul and will be suspended for the next game (no matter, it's only Chelsea). The momentum is firmly with our opponents now but with time almost up Gavin McCann somehow finds the energy to break from midfield and slides the ball invitingly into the path of the only bloke who can keep up with him, Gabby. He toe-pokes it past the 'keeper but agonizingly, inches wide of the post. Maybe he needs resting – that one would have gone in a month ago. We may not have deserved to win but we most definitely don't deserve what happens next as following a goalmouth scramble Bryan Hughes bundles in a late winner for Charlton.

This is probably our last chance of a point before we play Watford in three weeks. We're twelfth now, and although there's plenty of daylight between us and West Ham at the top of the bottom three, you just know they'll stay up. It's now officially squeaky-bum time. Don't you just love new-footie clichés?

The train home is a subdued affair, although the almighty storms that break as we head out of Euston provide a talking point. I later hear that several matches are abandoned due to the heavy rain, and if we'd have been kicking off at three o'clock things might have been interesting.

Chapter 7

Hey big spender

2nd January

Chelsea (home)

All our experienced players are either running on empty, carrying injuries or suspended. Confidence is low among the kids so they offer enthusiasm and little else. Both goalkeepers deemed good enough for the first team are out injured, replaced by a man in pyjamas, and we're up against a team whose reserves could beat our strongest side. As you can tell I'm not hopeful and my mood isn't helped when after five minutes I realise I'm sat next to a bloke who goes the toilet more than George Michael. Since our fourth member decided to hand back his season ticket we've had a gap in the middle of our little sewing circle. This is usually fine because more often than not the seat's empty or else the unlucky occupant moves along one so that the three survivors are still together. Unfortunately, the twice a season brigade tend not to know the rules and insist on sitting in the seat they've paid for – the very idea. So we get ninety minutes of him getting up and interrupting our conversation. Lord Justice Taylor has a lot to answer for.

Early in the game Freddie Bouma tackles Shaun Wright-Phillips with such timing and ferocity that it inspires his teammates and the tone is set. From that moment on this broken-down Villa team plays like their lives depend on keeping a clean sheet, and they restrict one of the best sides in Europe to a few fleeting chances.

Harassing Chelsea's millionaires and fighting for every ball, they give us a telling insight into just how good a manager Martin O'Neill is. He's with them in spirit, jumping about like a firecracker in his technical area, shouting, cajoling, berating officials, and no doubt like me, watching with a growing sense of pride in his makeshift Villa. Jose Mourinho, meanwhile, must be wondering if he ever will beat the Villa in a league game.

First we match them and then begin to dominate as the game goes on. Martin even makes the cheekiest of substitutions, bringing on Milan Baros in place of Steven Davis as we chased the win with 15 minutes to go. To Sky viewers it might be quite dull but to me it's anything but, and as the final whistle sounds it feels like not just a point, but also a turning point.

Watching the highlights on TV later I notice something I'd suspected but couldn't really see from our vantage point in the North Stand – Chelsea's following was pitiful. When their team starred Nigel Spackman and Doug Rougvie they'd fill the away end and almost any other part of the ground they fancied. Now they're the league champions they bring maybe a thousand-odd. Perhaps Roman should think of buying a few fans.

7th January
Manchester United (away)

It's tradition that cup draws are as kind to us as the Ugly Sisters were to Cinderella, and it seems we'll never go to the ball. This year the ghost of Bert Millichip haunts us again and sends us to Old Trafford to play Manchester United in the third round for the third time in six years.

I'm glad it's on the telly as I won't be going – it's one place where I get so wound up by the opposing fans there's every likelihood I'll get myself arrested. Last time I went it was all I could do to stop myself climbing over the fence into their section as they ridiculed us by singing "*We wanna be together*" in cod-Birmingham accents. Something about the hundreds of Brummie Reds no doubt joining in with this chant got right up my nose, and the inevitable defeats don't help either. One thing

I've noticed about Brummie Reds is that they're not just ninety-minute Mancs. They always talk Birmingham down and praise the Third City. To complete the loathsomeness profile, they more often than not say they've got a *"soft spot"* for Birmingham City. Which leads me on to another rant. Despite our mutual hatred, every Villa supporter I know has more time, in private at least, for a match-going Nose than they have for a stay-at-home Anywhere-But-Manchester Red. Is this compliment returned? You know the answer to that one.

Following on from Chelsea, it's another battling display and we come from behind to be level after ninety minutes. Gabby, as ever, showed no fear and even Baros was for once on top of his game. But as soon the fourth official checks Fergie's watch and holds up an added-time board that reads '4' I begin to fear the worst. Sure enough, Gabor Kiraly lets in a shot from Solskjaer that he could have just as easily thrown his cap on. Fifty years of hurt continues.

Oh well, we'd have lost the replay anyway and the lads look like they could do with a rest. That, more than anything, shows how low in public esteem the FA Cup has sunk. Third round day used to be the highlight of the season but now it's an after-thought, tacked on to mark the end of Sky's super, sensational, soaraway Christmas holiday extravaganza.

10th January

I'm always in a bad mood the day after we get knocked out of the cup, but Kerri comes into the front room with a copy of the *Mail.* "*Have you seen this?*"

Splashed over the front page is a story that you dream of reading, but never truly believe will happen. Birmingham City have had their official diary published, including their honours – seven league titles, seven FA Cups, five League Cups and the European Cup. And if that isn't funny enough, their official response, apart from wanting to know why the *Mail* is doing its job and reporting the best story in the city all year, includes the phrase: "*We would also like to make it clear that Birmingham City Football Club has never won the European Cup.*" So that's that one sorted.

11th January

Our paper-thin squad becomes even thinner with the departure of Didier Agathe. He came, he came on half a dozen times as a sub, but he didn't really go anywhere and now he's gone completely.

13th January
Manchester United (away)

Groundhog Day, and same as last week the boys will have to do without me. "*You've only come to see United*" is a chant the Old Trafford prawn munchers will never be able to aim Pennell-wards. Instead I opt to watch it at the Fordbridge Social with the usual collection of misfits who support a team from eighty miles away in order to feel good about their otherwise sad, failed lives. And some Blues they've loaned for the day.

In contrast to last week it's a mismatch from the start and we only begin to play well when United are three up and switch off. Gabby nets a consolation goal for us and that's Stamford Bridge, Anfield and now Old Trafford he's scored at, all before his 21st birthday. Some players never manage that in their entire careers but this level-headed lifelong Villa fan is good and getting better. It's a straw; start clutching. A more tangible straw is the fact that we've now played the top four clubs away so our record might start improving.

Just as an aside, over 150,000 have watched the Villa in the past seven days. That must be some sort of a record.

20th January
Watford (home)

There's talk about how this is the worst run in history (every Villa manager has to have a Worst Run In History, as well as a

Worst Performance For Twenty Years). Just as well that we've got Watford at home. A fantastic and gratefully received offer of six extra tickets for a fiver each is snapped up and I watch the match with my youngest son Tyler and my in-laws. Phil Bardsley, on loan from Manchester United, makes his debut and looks impressive, but to get out of our recent slump we need more than just a good right-back.

The atmosphere before the game is like a throwback to twelve months ago. Supporters are turning up out of routine rather than anticipation of seeing something truly exciting. I try to raise the spirits of everyone I speak to by pointing out that Real Madrid circa 1960 would have struggled if they'd had our injury problems and enthusing about the emerging genius of Gabby Agbonlahor, but there's still a fatality around the ground as we take our places. It's hard going at first as the team struggle to break down a doomed Watford side, for whom star player Ashley Young is absent due to a conflict of interests dilemma, brought on by the fact that next week he'll be playing for us.

Things improve a bit when Patrik Berger, just back from his loan spell at Stoke, comes on and shows what we've been missing by putting Baros through one-on-one with the keeper three times. He fluffs them all however and hopefully, unlike Young, won't be playing for us next week. We're being strongly linked with John Carew of Lyon and surely this is the biggest hint given to a Villa striker since Bosko Balaban arrived for training to find a plane ticket stuck in his boot. Baros finally goes off with ten minutes to go to a rousing chorus of boos the like of which hasn't been heard directed to a Villa player for a long, long time.

Myself, my own family and my extended Villa family breath a huge sigh of relief when Small Heathen Gavin Mahon deflects a McCann shot into his own goal, then in added time Gabby shows Baros how it should be done – 2-0.

The youth team and a few old heads have battled gamely to this point in the season, but with eleven days until the transfer deadline, it's time to send for reinforcements. We finish the game with Gabby and Berger up front and Baros and Angel in the dressing room, so it's clear to see where Martin O'Neill will be looking to strengthen.

22nd January

Here's a thing. Lee Hendrie, on the bench after briefly returning from Stoke, stands accused of insulting a disabled Manchester United supporter up at Old Trafford. This sort of thing makes me smile; supporters dish out all sorts of insults to players then act like nuns when a player has a go back. Lee denies he said anything, I for one believe him – not even Hendrie would be daft enough to have a go at the disabled section, particularly at a ground where searching for ways to become offended has become an art form – and someone's got their name in the papers. Good for them

29th January

And now for a bit of good news. Roy Aitken, last seen leaving Villa Park as Martin strolled in, has been appointed assistant manager of Scotland. And there'll be no jokes here about him giving up football for good. Aitken always got roped in with O'Leary when the stick was handed out, but to his eternal credit he held the playing staff together during the chaos that surrounded the Clueless One's departure and made things a lot easier for Martin when he arrived. Just to make it a bit harder he was recovering after an operation to remove a brain tumour at the time and it's difficult to express how much respect you can give to a man like that.

31st January
Newcastle United (away)

Two years ago our last-day arrival consisted of Eric Djemba-Djemba, following in the footsteps of such January signings as Joey Gudjonsson and Nolberto Iscariot. Last year's big January news was to decide we couldn't afford Eirik Bakke's wages. This season the cavalry arrives in the shape of John Carew and diminutive Ashley Young. Leaving are Peter Whittingham to Cardiff and Milan Baros to Lyon in exchange for Big John. The former Valencia striker has done the business on the big stage and a straight swap for a man who's been as much use as a glass hammer since the previous manager signed him has to represent good business.

Young is a gamble, having played only twenty Premier League games, but the £8 million fee (possibly rising to a Villa record £9.65 million), hints at our spending power under Randy. You don't splash that kind of cash on 'potential' if you can't afford to spend even more if it doesn't work out. Many times under Doug we lost out because we waited until the selling club dropped their price. This time we've said, *"Okay – what do you want? Done."* There's also reports we've signed a pre-contract with Celtic's Shaun Maloney. I've only seen him briefly, playing for Celtic against Man United, but I was impressed.

The acid test of course is on the pitch, and both new boys make their debut against Newcastle, whose manager Glenn Roeder adds spice to the fixture by questioning O'Neill's courage for turning down the job that Roeder himself was pleased to accept. No wonder – as the unlikely achievement of getting the best West Ham side for twenty years relegated suggests, he couldn't manage his dinner and would probably take any job that doesn't involve asking *"Do you want fries with that?"*

It's a long, long way to Newcastle so naturally we get scheduled to play there midweek. I wasn't going, but Dave rings me with news of a spare so I explain to Kerri that I'm helping him out and jump into the car for our northern expedition.

Everyone likes to scoff at Newcastle's nineties resurgence, when forty thousand previous conscientious objectors enrolled as lifelong members of the Toon Army. The truth is they were getting low crowds when they were doing badly and started getting bigger crowds when things began to look up, just like every club does. That's what we have to do; make people think the good times are just around the corner. Of course, it helps that Newcastle are a hundred miles from civilisation as well. They've got no rivals for potential supporters as the only other big team up there are Sunderland, and nobody from one of those two cities is going to support anything from the other. So, all we have to do is persuade our sceptical fanbase we really are going to win the league next year, and possibly bomb St Andrew's, the Hawthorns and Molineux.

Newcastle fly out of the traps, roared on by fifty thousand pot-bellied blokes, and are two goals up after just seven minutes. The Villa defence are like rabbits in headlights and Young and Carew must be wondering what they've let themselves in for. Gradually however, we get a foothold in the game and begin to apply some pressure on the ropey Toon rearguard. A loose ball from a corner is lashed home by Young and from here on in the game is as one-sided as a Zimbabwean election.

Carew, whose agility and speed belie his physique, sees a header hit the woodwork and is unlucky with a fine volley. There's controversy when he has a good goal disallowed for pushing, when everyone but the ref saw it was the Norwegian being fouled. The constant Villa pressure subsides when the man-mountain is withdrawn, and although we still push for an equaliser the inevitable happens when we're caught on the break and concede a third. It's a sickening blow, but the Villa have given such an exhilarating glimpse of things to come, with the debutants performing so well, that defeat is easier to take.

As we leave the ground I see a stunningly beautiful young woman arm-in-arm with a Toon army stereotype in a replica shirt that probably didn't fit him when Malcolm MacDonald was playing. She certainly didn't fit Fat Freddy Shepherd's description of Newcastle women as dogs – in fact, the last time I saw a woman that pretty on a Geordie's arm it was a tattoo.

Listening to *Five Live* on the way home, news breaks that we've beaten the midnight transfer deadline to sign Shaun

Maloney for a million quid rather than wait until the summer to get him for nothing. Apart from Ashley Young, every player O'Neill has brought to the Villa has Champions League experience. That can only bode well for the future and it's the reason why, despite tonight's defeat, I'll sleep soundly when we finally get back to England.

Chapter 8

Unfamiliar friends

2nd February

There I was, sitting at home watching the news when instead of the usual impartial, unbiased BBC reporting they started spouting some gibberish about Gareth Barry being called up to the England squad. What's the world coming to when even the BBC start talking utter nonsense?

3rd February
West Ham (home)

Another of life's imponderables – why do our crowds always get bigger after Christmas? Thanks in no small measure to the new signings (it can't be the results), the feelgood factor is slowly returning to B6. I sell more *H&Vs* than I have for a couple of years, witness people walking towards the ground with smiles on their faces for the first time in weeks and there are over 41,000 inside Villa Park. A rare 3 o'clock Saturday kick-off helps, as does the free travel laid on for the West Ham fans by their chairman. Bloody smalltime clubs, having to have their travel paid by some rich foreigner.

Villa start well enough, with Young and Carew continuing where they left off against Newcastle. The pair have quickly built an understanding of each other's play and one slick move between them ends with the Norwegian giant scoring on his home debut.

The Hammers' own new signing, Matthew Upson, is being led a merry dance and after just half an hour he goes off injured, possibly with twisted blood. As he limps towards the dressing room one cruel fan behind me shouts: *"Oi Curbishley! When the rest of you get in there he'll have put candles all round the bath!"*

Villa continue to press but can't score the killer goal, though you'd need a micrometer to measure how far Berger had strayed offside for his disallowed effort. He'd come on for Carew with twenty minutes left and although I'd have kept our newest cult hero on to hold the ball up and kick the opposition, he was clearly knackered.

With about ten minutes to go West Ham finally realise it's not a game of attackers v. defenders and launch a frantic assault on the Villa goal, desperate for a point in their battle against the drop. There's lots of pinball but precious little wizardry, and what there is comes from Tommy Sorenson. Dave, who's been unnaturally quiet all afternoon, gets very animated about a goalmouth scramble during which our oft-criticised goalkeeper makes two miraculous saves. This, I'm sure, is completely unrelated to the fact that a new *H&V* sells better after the match if we haven't given away a late equaliser. It's three points and some much needed breathing space over the Premiership's cellar-dwellers. West Ham are truly awful and seemingly in need of a miracle to save them.

Later, the vertically challenged owner of another club who has recently been critical of his own supporters has this to say about their local rivals: *"The club down the road, having won once in fourteen games, plays a club third from bottom of the league, and get nearly 42,000. How can we compete against them and their support?"*

The answer is you can't. After 130 years you'd have thought it would have sunk in by now.

7th February

At first I assumed the telly was broke, or I was having some weird hallucogenic dream. But no, I heard right first time. Our Gareth is indeed playing for England, or at least on the bench for a friendly with Spain. He gets on for the second half and for the first time since Darius Vassell was playing for them I watch an England game with anything other than total disinterest. With right-footed Gary Neville at left-back and central midfielder Frank Lampard on the left wing it was only natural that the most consistent left-footed English player should be in the middle, but where would we be if Steve McLaren used logic? Barry did all the right things, looked tidy enough, didn't give the ball away, so he'll never play for England again. They lost 1-0, for anyone who's interested in that sort of thing.

10th February
Reading (away)

The turning point I thought had been reached after the draw with Chelsea has proved elusive, although to be fair the fixture list from hell hasn't helped. So it's with fragile confidence we set off for the Madjeski Stadium to face Reading, who are flying up the table after four successive victories.

The good football they played in their Villa Park defeat at the start of the season has proved to be no fluke, and they've adapted to life in the Premier League far better than most promoted sides. Credit for this must go to Steve Coppell, who over the years has shown himself to be an efficient organiser of teams and a perceptive spotter of talented players. Good job too as, let's face it, he was never going to make it as a comedian was he?

It's been snowing for a couple of days in Birmingham – two inches on Friday brought the city to a halt – but there's no problem down in the sunny south so the game's on. I'm on the Chiltern line with Dave Woodley, who I've known since we were both about seven. Dave last missed a league game in 1982 and he's a world expert on train fares so with a combination of cheap day returns and travel cards the fare's about £25, which is a lot less than getting an ordinary ticket. Sometimes it pays to have your own anorak.

We get the bus to the ground and gaze in awe at... another

identikit out of town Leisure Experience. There's a hotel, a KFC, Pizza Hut, and a football ground somewhere as well. I'm inside before all this rampant consumerism sparks off a Marxist Revolutionary Frenzy.

Another Saturday in another bowl. The sign saying "*Please Be Aware of Flying Footballs*" causes a wry smile but the game follows a worryingly similar pattern to the Newcastle encounter, and we fall behind early on following some 'after you' marking straight from the David O'Leary coaching manual. Naturally it's scored by Steve Sidwell, who is living proof that English football doesn't end with the Premiership. From then on we spend the rest of the game camped in the Reading half, although you have to wonder if this is kudos to us, or because our opponents are happy to concede possession as long as we appear incapable of making it count.

John Carew has a monumental tussle with his marker Bikey all afternoon, but Gabby and Ashley Young miss some decent chances before Reading wrap up the three points with a flowing move as time is running out – Sidwell again. He's been a dominant force in Reading's season and with his contract running out in the summer we could do a lot worse than kidnap him and take him back to Villa Park. I hope he doesn't decide to join Manchester United or Chelsea; it does no-one any good if a player of Sidwell's quality plays three cup games and makes a couple of ten-minute substitute appearances a season.

We're thirteenth – no danger of relegation but not much chance of improvement the way things are going. I think I'm beginning to understand what Kevin Keegan meant when he said, "*I know we'll turn the corner, I just don't know where the corner is.*"

The crowd is given as 24,122; Reading's highest of the season. Judging by the reaction of the home supporters nearest to us, the odd 122 of them don't watch *Soccer AM*. My idealistic belief that we are all born equal is severely challenged when confronted by a grown man wearing a jester's hat and a football shirt, waving his arms and shouting "*Easy, easy.*"

At the end of the match we could always stay behind to proclaim our undying love for Aston Villa and its players. Or we could nip out sharpish and catch the first bus back to the station. Pragmatism wins out over loyalty and both Dave and I can show a turn of speed that belies our appearance when it comes to missing the traffic. The 77 is just filling up nicely as we nip onboard and pulls away almost immediately. There's not much traffic around and we get back to the station in time for the first train and home just turned six. Early kick-offs can have their uses.

As Dave gets off the train at Dorridge I look at him and think here's someone I've known for years, yet all I know is his name and the fact that he supports the Villa and has a love of loud punky rock music. I don't know where he lives, what he does for a living, the names of any of his family or what he thinks about the Common Agricultural Policy. I've spent many a day with him, shared experiences good, bad, indifferent and terrfying, he's one of my oldest friends and yet I don't really know anything about him. Moreover, I know dozens like him and so does every football supporter of our generation regardless of who they support.

Chapter 9

Never neutral

3rd March
Fulham (away)

A combination of our usual early cup exit and an international break means it's been three weeks since our last game. There's no doubt that the rest will benefit some of our players; Gabby in particular is showing signs of battle fatigue having played every minute of every game until his substitution at Reading. On the other hand our new signings could do with more games to attain fitness and a better understanding of each other's play.

We have no-one but ourselves to blame for cup exits, but blank weekends for international games are the ones that really hack me off. Waking up on a Saturday with nothing to look forward to but an army of part-time football experts turning up in the pub is not my idea of fun. Clogging up the bar and going on about how England only have to turn up on time to win the World Cup, they'd get more respect from me if they actually went to the games, but that would take too much time and effort, not to mention beer money.

Still the long break has certainly created an appetite among Villa fans to see their heroes in action and we've snapped up all our own tickets, most of the 'neutral zone', and even a few in the home sections of Craven Cottage. A further sign of the eagerness of our fans is that all the old Chelmsley Villa have hired a coach, our first since the League Cup semi-final at Everton in 1984. I won't go into detail about what happened there, suffice to say it got a mention in *Villains*, and also Crimewatch's Greatest Hits Volume One.

The coach leaves the White Hart at 9.30am, and a couple of Blues fans turn up to see if we've filled it. The word you're looking for, yet again, is 'obsessed'. Not only is our coach full to bursting, we've also got a mini-bus in tow with only one space on it, and that's because my mate Dave Nolan hasn't turned up. I ring him to see where he is. When he finally answers I can tell immediately by his croaky voice that he won't be coming.

"Are you up yet?" I ask, and I can almost feel the hangover myself as he answers, *"I've only just got in."* He's never been a morning person. If only I'd known that was the last time I'd ever talk to him.

The organisers had to say to the coach hire firm that we were day trippers rather than football fans in order to avoid being forced to the ground early and home straight after by police. But it's only when we're well underway that I find out the coach is not due to leave London until 10.30pm, which in reality means well after midnight and a three o'clock arrival in downtown Chelmsley. This in turn means that having left Kerri babysitting and promising she could go out on my return, I have to start thinking about making my own way back.

We park up at Perrivale station, within sight of the slowly-increasing Wembley arch, and take the tube to Earl's Court, where we go into the first pub we see and settle down to watch the Liverpool v. Man United game in the company of a few Cockney Reds of both persuasions. They're like an irritating rash aren't they? They get everywhere.

We decide to move closer to the ground and re-board the tube to Putney Bridge, where outside the station the Eight Bells is rammed solid. So too is the rather unfortunately named Zulu Bar, which is where we spend the last bit of drinking time before the match. Here we encounter another rift between the young and old Villa support. The youth wail some unmusical dirge about Carew being on fire whilst the classic rock element still believe Brian Little walks on water.

After about twenty minutes Carew, Carew, Carew is on fire as he puts us in front with a deft finish but the lead hardly outlasts the celebrations as Fulham equalise thanks to some slack marking for a change. Nothing much happens for the rest of the game but that doesn't fully explain why many home fans find the traveling support more watchable than the game. The support from our contingent is simply awesome and there are times when I fear the stand might collapse into the Thames a few yards behind us. Afternoons like this remind me that no matter how quiet Villa Park might sometimes be, we're up with the best on our travels.

Another day, another draw, but a it's valuable point that maintains a nice gap with the teams below us. It's hardly a royal wedding but we raise a glass or two anyway before I cadge a lift on a mini-bus that's going almost my way. Unfortunately, apart from a few honourable exceptions (the Turners and the Gambles) the passengers seem to be from the Tracey Andrews Appreciation Society, Combat 18 Branch, so when I finally get home the twinkling lights of Chelmsley Wood have never looked so welcoming.

14th March
Arsenal (home)

It's been six weeks since our last home match and our editor is suffering. His emergency DSS loan has been turned down so he's had no alternative but to lay off his footman and the maid is on a three-day week. Luckily we've got a game tonight so Bob Geldof won't be needed.

Whenever we play Arsenal I'm reminded of the time a few years ago when I was selling *H&V* on Trinity Road. On this particular occasion the club were flying a '1981 League Champions' flag from the Trinity Road stand, and some Gooners sitting near me on the grass were mocking the age of the flag.

"We were flying our European Cup Winners flag last week," I

said, and they just stared at me, open-mouthed. *"You haven't got one of those have you, you slack-jawed morons?"* This was before Dave sent all his sellers on customer relations courses obviously.

We get off to a bad start when a shot is deflected past the help-less Sorenson by Eboue, who is yards offside. Just recently it seems that if it wasn't for bad luck we wouldn't get any kind of luck at all (which comes from *Born Under A Bad Sign*, co-writ-ten by Booker T, of & the MGs fame, trivia fans). After that we play quite well against an admittedly understrength Arsenal side, but are repeatedly frustrated in our efforts to break them down, and let down again by poor finishing. Carew is brought down on the edge of the area but we're playing a Big Club so a sending-off isn't an option. Yet again Arsenal try to walk the ball into the net; if Henry was playing they'd have been four up at half-time.

With half an hour left we can see there won't be any more goals, Arsenal can't be bothered to attack anymore and we've run out of ideas. Maybe Martin O'Neill isn't the managerial superman we heralded him as after all. That afternoon on the North Stand car park seems a long time ago and I spend a few minutes wondering why you don't get dogs running on the pitch like you used to. It used to happen all the time didn't it? The match would be going on then a dog would run on the pitch and do a lap or two of the mud-churned midfield before being caught by a goalkeeper or jovial referee Roger Kirkpatrick (Leicester) and handed over to a police sergeant. And how, after all these years, can I still remember Roger Kirkpatrick came from Leicester?

As the game fizzles out the strains of an unfamiliar ditty make themselves known from the back of the Holte End. It takes a while to realise it's that lovable tune of peace and reconciliation *Ten German Bombers*, presumably aimed at Arsenal keeper Jens Lehmann. Even Ingerlund's finest have given up on this one now so why do we wheel it out? Whatever happened to singing about the team?

The defeat leaves us still thirteenth in the league, but with teams below us starting to pick up points these are worrying times. It would be a tragedy if, after finally getting rid of Baron Hard-up, the glorious new era that surely beckons is postponed for a couple of years by relegation.

18th March
Liverpool (home)

From the time Aston Villa invented league football right up until a few years ago, you were at home one week, away the next, and there was still time to fit in as many cup replays as were necessary. It wasn't hard to understand, but that was when a bloke with a pencil worked out the fixtures. Nowadays it's all done on a computer so we get the annoying habit of having to play twice away then twice at home. No wonder attendances at some clubs are suffering.

Take our recent run for instance. Two away games three weeks apart, followed by a trio of home matches. Today is the first part of a Scouse double-bill, so I'll need eyes in the back of my head and a keen awareness of moody £20 notes. Turnstile operators may have to keep a similar look-out for dodgy tickets, as the visit of Liverpool attracts a capacity crowd and when Scousers can't get tickets they just do a Blue Peter – *"Here's one I made earlier, la."*

After saying that, there's a strange phenomenon amongst football supporters. Manchester United get justified stick for being Cockneys while Liverpool have all the Scouse clichés thrown at them, when in fact they've got even more out of town support than their red brethren. I find Liverpool supporters slightly less irritating than United's. They've got the arrogance, but at least they can back it up with something a bit more tangible than *"We're the biggest club in the world. We are you know. We really are. Your team's rubbish."* I still wouldn't let my daughter marry one, mind.

With the weather being unseasonably sunny before the game I decided to ignore the forecaster's advice and wear a rather stylish and, though I say it myself, pretty damned sexy Fred Perry number. Two hours later, with the skies darkening and snow flurries whipping across Aston Park, I'd have happily traded style for one of those manager's jackets that look daft but keep you warm. It was eventually a relief to get into the sheltered, and full to capacity, Villa Park ready for an appetising contest between the up and coming Aston Villa and the former Kings of Europe.

The match itself is hardly worth the price of a photocopy with both sides happy to settle for a point. Judging by his decision not to award a penalty when Petrov is fouled by two Reds defenders at once, the referee is also content with a draw. Maybe we're the last game on his fixed odds from yesterday, or perhaps we used our quota of successful penalty appeals earlier in the season. I don't usually notice the opposition, but Liverpool are awful. All the money they've spent and they can't come up with anything better than this dross. If I supported them I'd be demanding to know why a team who can beat Barcelona play like this a few days later.

The only point of interest in the first 89 minutes comes when a Liverpool supporter in the North Stand, contrary to the rules of etiquette when straying where you shouldn't be, stands up to applaud the arrival of Robbie Fowler into the proceedings. You can always tell a part-timer; regulars in the wrong part of the ground because they can't get a ticket in with their own fans keep their gobs shut for ninety minutes. Mrs Hunter's lad Glory at his one match a season has to show the world who he supports. There's a bit of shouting and he gets advised to leave by one of the stewards. Sitting in the wrong end is, of course, a serious crime unless it's you who's doing it. Then it's acceptable and the home team's fault for not being able to sell all their tickets. Long live double standards.

Fowler, who for the past ten years has regarded games against

Villa as more like testimonials, misses a last minute chance that denies our more excitable supporters the opportunity to do their final meerkat impersonation of the season and the final whistle goes to end a horrible match in conditions that suited. I wish I'd worn my big coat.

Sad statistic time – we haven't beaten Liverpool at home for nine years. We haven't beaten Manchester United at all since August 1995. Some of that is because they've been demonstrably better than us in the time, but a lot of the time, especially against Liverpool, we've had an inferiority complex even when our team has obviously been as good as theirs. I'd hoped the draws we got at Arsenal and Chelsea at the start of the season would have given us some self-belief but in the last two matches you can still see the team's confidence drain as soon as they get into the opposition half.

Before the game most of my customers, no doubt impressed by Liverpool's Champions League win in Barcelona, had predicted a Villa defeat. Even so callers to radio phone-ins on the way home are still moaning as Charlton have won, so effectively we are two points closer to the bottom three than we were this morning. Personally, I still think Martin O'Neill is a genius but there are a lot more dissenting voices than there used to be. It's a worrying time.

22nd March

Today marks a significant moment in the modern history of Aston Villa, namely, we have to make another decision on what was the worst performance for twenty years. This honour has traditionally been granted to the 5-0 debacle away at Southampton in 1987 as a matter of routine but yesterday was the twentieth anniversary of that one, so we've got to find another. I give the matter some thought before deciding on the 3-0 defeat away at Charlton in April 1987. In another month's time I can think about it a bit more.

24th March

If Martin O'Neill didn't think he'd been accepted as a Villa man before, he knows he's made it now. Andy Gray, who managed to walk out of his 'first love' three times, pausing only to stab as many backs as he could manage, states that Villa under Martin O'Neill are sliding into trouble.

I never know what to make of Gray. Granted, he was one of my first Villa heroes, and that team of 1977 he starred in is still the best team I've ever watched. But he seems to have an issue with every manager there's ever been, with the exception of his mate Ron. Does he want the job himself? And if so, why did he choose to work for Sky when he was Atkinson's assistant and natural successor. This is the sort of in-depth discussion I find myself having with Wes most days, which is just as well otherwise I'd spent a lot of time talking to myself. It's not as though there's anything else to do during work hours.

28th March

The new season ticket prices are announced, and this is good news for our employer, who generously buys ours at the start of the season. The North Stand is down to £300, which has to be the best value in the Premier League. It's high enough to see everything, close to the pitch and the legroom isn't really an issue.

30th March

As advertised on the Villa website:

"Partnership Activation Executive

With a strong background in partner activation within the Sport Marketing arena, you'll assist in creating opportunities for partnerships, create marketing opportunities and maintain regular contact with Aston Villa's corporate clients... The successful applicant is likely to have a background in Sports marketing or similar, particularly in relation to Partnerships Activation."

That's the job advert appearing on the club website, so naturally I send in my CV. I don't think two O levels and a first-class honours degree from the University of Life gives me much hope but it's better than breaking pallets. I wouldn't mind a career activating partnerships.

Chapter 10

Werewolf's return

2nd April

Everton (home)

You meet all sorts standing outside football grounds. I met Kerri when I used to sell *H&V* on Trinity Road. She was working as a volunteer for St. John's Ambulance at the time, and I seem to remember suffering a lot of migraines and sprained ankles that season. Over the years my customers have been a diverse array of characters, including *Five Live*'s Pat Murphy, Lisa Smith of the *Birmingham Mail*, Greatest Living Brummie Carl Chinn, hoolie-legend Black Danny, Barney out of Napalm Death, Simon Inglis, Tom Hanks and Prince William. (I made a couple up).

Tonight I'm shooting the pleasant spring breeze with Neil Moxley of the *Daily Mail* and the *Guardian*'s Stuart James, who want to know what the rank and file think of Villa's recent results and performances. After making it clear I speak for no-one but myself, which is compulsory when making such statements lest the wrath of the internet gurus be unleashed, I suggest we're suffering from a crisis of confidence that has reduced any kind of tactical plan to a big boot in the general direction of John Carew.

What we need is the influence of players who aren't afraid to do something with the ball, like Patrik Berger and Shaun Maloney, who haven't figured much in the team recently. Tonight's game illustrates my point so perfectly that I expect a mention in tomorrow's match reports.

The first half is awful, with Villa treating the ball like a hand-grenade with the pin pulled out until it could be launched for Carew to chase. Gavin McCann is symptomatic of the current malaise, winning every tackle but then defeating the object by continually giving the ball back to Everton. The only spark of inspiration comes from some young lad who runs onto the pitch from the Holte, pulls a ball out of his pocket and lashes it into the back of the net. As we go in at half-time trailing to a goal from supposed Villa fan Jolean Lescott, we are booed off for, as far as I recall, the first time this season. It isn't an entirely undeserved response to the performance.

Lescott and the missing Tim Cahill are cases in point. Neither of them were unknowns, they'd been in the lower divisions for years and they were within reach of even Doug's anemic transfer budget. Yet while David O'Leary cursed about his small squad, honest bunches of lads and the restrictions he was working under, David Moyes was taking a gamble on players like that and putting together a team that look headed for Europe.

The second half is a different story as we start to play something resembling football after McCann's withdrawal and get a late equaliser from Gabby. Maloney plays well but Berger is inspired, and you start to think that after two seasons of injuries and arguments he's finally earning his wages. Earlier in the season he was exiled to Stoke after allegedly refusing to prove his fitness in the reserves, and while O'Neill was absolutely right not to tolerate such an affront to his authority, you can't help but wonder where we'd be if the talented Czech had been available for selection during our bad run. Not looking to see how Charlton have got on, that's for sure. You also wonder what might have happened if Lee Hendrie, another loanee to the Britannia Stadium, had got his act together in the same way. Then again, we've been thinking that for five years or more-without any explanation.

6th April (Good Friday)

Taking advantage of the school holidays, me, my son Tyler and Kerri's little sister Olivia go on the stadium tour. It's a chance to explore all the little nooks and crannies of our beautiful ground that you never normally get to see, and very impressive it is too. Some of the historical inaccuracies, as recited by the tour guide, are a little annoying though. For instance, founder of the Football League William MacGregor is described as a turnstile operator who ended up on the board, when in fact he was a visionary whose idea it was to rope off the ground and charge admission. I point a few errors out but the guide gets annoyed after a bit so I keep quiet for the rest of the tour and wallow in nostalgia and pride. They should give me a job here.

But all in all, it's a nice day out for the kids and good value for money too, with lunch in the Corner Flag thrown in at a total cost of just over twenty quid. Also having a meal in the pitch-side restaurant is Steve Stride, and we have a long chat as I get to thank him personally for all the hard work he's put in on behalf of the Villa over the years. A talented administrator and one of the good guys, even though the rent-a-gob brigade ridiculed him as an Ellis lackey. He will be sorely missed when he retires at the end of the season.

7th April
Blackburn Rovers (away)

Up the M6 nice and early today for the annual Blackburn pub-crawl which includes a pint in the Golden Cup (which used to be a nice quiet place until they built a motorway junction next to it making it both the first pub off the motorway and also within walking distance of the ground), another in the Bear Hotel, and about a gallon in the Fernhurst. It seems a lot of Villa supporters have the same idea and I'm not sure how to explain it but judging by the support today and at Fulham recently you'd think we were going for the title rather than living in fear of the drop.

There's a lot of old school lads in the Fernhurst, paying tribute to one of their number, Steve Norton, who died twelve months ago. Not only is it the anniversary of his death, but the last away he attended was at Blackburn. Steve was a decent bloke, kept himself to himself but always around the scene. When people like that go it makes you wonder what the future holds for the rest of us.

Fair play to Blackburn for encouraging away supporters with cheap tickets, and to a couple of their fans I spoke to for acknowledging us as the best following they'd seen all season and commenting how nice it would be to watch a match with an atmosphere for a change.

Team selection is a bit of a puzzle, with no Carew or McCann, but the performance is every bit as good as the support. Despite going behind thanks to Bardsley rashly giving away a penalty, we control the game for long periods and Berger, who equalises with a deft flick on his first start of the season, is particularly outstanding. Freddie Bouma looks a different player from last season and Craig Gardner's energy and commitment surely signals the end of McCann's time in the middle of the pitch. Gareth Barry plays like our very own version of Gerrard or Lampard in central midfield and Martin Laursen is the player he can always be.

Whatever our injury problems might have been they were obviously nothing on Blackburn's as they've had to rope in some bloke out of the pie queue. I think his name's David Dunn and although he tries his best it's plain to see that he isn't a proper footballer as he helps Berger set up Gabby for the winner. At the final whistle the team come over to the Darwen End to celebrate and throw shirts into the ecstatic mass of humanity therein. We're still only seven points away from the drop zone but with six games to go that should be enough.

A good away win in front of a great following like today's is the best thing in football, but I can't rejoice too much as a combination of alcohol, sunshine, fags, singing and travel leaves me with the worst case ever of a phenomenon many of you will know only too well – the football headache. We drive back down the M6 with me wishing the road wasn't so noisy. Luckily Kerri's gone out by the time I get home so I can head for bed undisturbed. When she gets back I'll be in a coma. Not tonight dear, I've got a headache.

9th April
Wigan Athletic (home)

When I gave up my seat for the Man United home game all those months ago, I had a contingency plan that failed miserably. I rang my mate Paul Hansaker, who owns a recruitment firm called PH Services, to ask if there was any room for me in his corporate box. Unfortunately, due to the glamorous opposition and the time of year he, rather selfishly I thought, wanted to use the occasion to invite his most valued customers and ply them with free booze... I mean treat them to some hospitality. "*You're welcome to come to a crap game,*" he said. "*Come against Wigan.*" Thanks a lot pal.

So it's from the refined heights of a balcony in the Witton Lane stand I witness the worst assault on a goalkeeper since Peter McParland retired resulting in Wigan taking the lead, as Emile Heskey manages to stay on his hooves long enough to poke the ball home. We lay siege to the Latics' goal (see, all those chats with proper journos have paid off) in search of an equaliser and finally get one when a Berger cross is deflected in by Gabby, seemingly with his wedding tackle. Oh well, they all count.

The perceived idea of the True Supporter is that they wouldn't want to be in a box because you miss out on the atmosphere and the 'banter' (horrible word) of being with your 'mates' (another *Soccer AM*-ism). Personally, given the choice of a free bar, food, unlimited class 'A' drugs, models swanning around and the opportunity to be in the warm when it's freezing cold outside, or sitting next to the group of misanthropes I have the misfortune to attend games with, pass me the prawn sandwiches and another brandy please.

Talking of the lower orders, the away fans are downstairs in Witton Lane again, which gives Villa supporters the bottom of the North Stand. Having our own support behind both goals will, apparently, make us unbeatable at home but it seems to have little effect today. It's £15 to get in there, which is about right given the appalling view and the lack of legroom, and I can't see it being full next season unless they keep the prices at that level.

In the bar after the game, I see that one of the waitresses is my old mate Gail from Chelmsley Wood, who I haven't seen for a while. At first I couldn't tell her out of civvies, but she recognised me straight away.

"What are you doing here?" she asks as we hug. *"Oh yeah, you're a Villa bastard int ya."*

You can take the girl out of Chelmsley...

10th April

Spurs reserves (home)

Once a season, under strict conditions, I attend a reserve game. It has to be at Villa Park (Bescot is no man's land after dark), there must be absolutely nothing worth watching on TV, even *UK Gold*, and I must have had a written guarantee from Shefali that it won't rain or be too cold from the moment I leave the house until I get back to my palatial mansion in the North Solihull stockbroker belt. Other clubs manage to package reserve games as Family Fun Nights, dragging in thousands of kids who'd rather be off joyriding and drinking alcopops, to have their faces painted and watch a collection of Academy prospects plus a few embittered old pros seeing out the last months of their contracts attempting to maim Academy prospects. We still can't get more than a couple of hundred scattered around the centre section of Trinity Rd.

We've been winning youth and reserve trophies regularly over the years but there isn't a lot to get impressed with tonight. Villa are beaten by a good-looking Spurs side who go two up just after half-time and are content to kill the game off from then, although we do get one back a few seconds from the end. Liam Ridgewell and Steven Davis look streets ahead of the rest, which is encouraging and disappointing in equal measures because I'd like to have been able to spot a youngster who was better than both of them. The only other player who stood out was Barry Bannon, a 4'3" midfielder destined for cult hero status until he gets released and slides down the leagues to end up the star of his local pub team. Whenever I see the kids playing I can't help being saddened by the fact that every single one of them believes he's destined to be a big name when the chances are that this is as good as it'll ever get. Being told that your best days are behind you at 17 must be crushing. My lads play football and while I'd love them to be good enough to play for the Villa I think that, on the whole, I'd rather they lived normal lives.

14th April
Middlesbrough (away)

Now our unbeaten run has removed any last worries about going down, Middlesbrough seems a long way to go for a game with not much to play for. Not only that, but I still have night-mares about Ayresome Park, where I once arrived a good hour before kick-off to find Boro's firm already waiting for us in the away end. That's great if you're Pete the Greek, but not so good when you're the youngest soldier (by about fifty years) in the Flask and Blanket Brigade that made up the Travellers Club.

So, having been up for work at quarter to five all week, I decide to stay in bed with Helen Chamberlain and follow the game on Sky. I met her once, when I got roped into taking part in a quiz on Sky's Sunday morning programme. My plans for the morning are as spoiled as mine were for the rest of her life, how-ever, when my upstairs neighbour starts vacuuming her wooden floor at 7.30, which in a council tower block is like a thunder-storm going off six feet above your head. Coma patients would-n't sleep through it. Being unemployed and frankly, unemploy-able, my neighbour has no concept of the weekend lie-in, her

only clue that it's Saturday being when Jeremy Kyle doesn't
come on.

We were destined not to get on when, soon after they moved in,
I heard her and her boyfriend jumping around and screeching
like excited chimps as Small Heath beat Norwich in the play-
offs. During one of many subsequent slanging matches, as she
let rip a tirade of foul-mouthed abuse in front of her young son
in his tatty blue kit, I threatened to report her to Social Services
if she continued to make the poor little beggar dress up in such
stupid clothes. That was when she told me that the lad's father
used to be a Villa fan until recently, but was now one of that lot,
and my contempt for them was complete.

Thanks to the acoustics of their ultra-cheap wooden floor, you
can hear every four-letter word when their voices are raised,
and me and the missus have nicknamed them Punch and Judy.
The rows, the beatings, the tears, the Domestic Violence Unit
banging on the door... and that's just when they're listening to
Tom Ross breakin' 'is 'eart. I once wrote them a polite note asking for a little consideration, pointing out that as a taxpayer, I'm
the mug who pays their rent and benefits and would appreciate
the chance to occasionally get some sleep when I'm on nights.
All to no avail, though to be fair I don't think reading is their
strong point and the only language they appear fluent in is
'offensive'.

They're even noisier than usual today, (it's either the mating
season or they're having a tea party), so I'm off up the pub for
some peace and quiet.

The White Hart is not the best place to watch football as all the
old boys usually insist on watching the horse racing. But one of
the lads has brought a universal remote control out with him and
we have great fun by turning over to the football scores just as
the races are entering the final furlong, much to the loudly-
expressed dismay of the degenerate gamblers.

Even more fun is the scoreline from the Riverside as we come
from behind yet again to win with goals from Gardner, Moore

and a particularly re-born Petrov. He's not had the best of starts to his Villa career and there's been all sorts of rumours he's back off to Celtic, with the obligatory nudge-wink references to drugs and Mrs Petrov's extra-curricular activities from internet nerds trying to impress fellow net nerds with their inside knowledge, but the past couple of games have seen him back on form.

As the three points take us into the top half of the table and page one on the Teletext tables (which is apparently quite important to the New Fans) it's hard to believe that only a fortnight ago we were anxiously looking over our shoulders at the drop zone. Not that I was ever worried.

17th April

There's been speculation about Juan Pablo Angel leaving almost since he arrived six years ago, so it comes as a surprise that he really has gone, to MLS club New York Red Bulls. I've always loved him but due to a combination of reasons he's never had the chance to show us what he could do over a period of time and at 31 he isn't going to have much opportunity now our forward line is starting to take shape. Even Angel's worst enemies couldn't deny he's conducted himself with the utmost professionalism in what's often been trying circumstances and never given less than his all. If only all big name foreign arrivals to the Premiership had the same attitude.

22nd April
Portsmouth (home)

The small rise in Villa Park attendances may not have been spectacular, but given the mood last summer which led to season ticket sales of only fifteen thousand, I dread to think what crowds might have been like were it not for the arrival of Randy and Martin. Having worked the streets of Aston on matchdays for eighteen years now, I have a pretty unique insight into the make up of our support, and I can promise you that a lot of old faces are returning to the fold.

Among them is the famous Werewolf, who's started coming down again after years of absence, and is today is accompanied by something that I would guess is a female of their particular species. *"Orriyttmayt,"* he grunts as they walk, paw-in-paw, towards Witton Lane, and worried parents clutch their children closer, telling them that it's rude to point and stare.

The game is a painfully dull goalless draw, remarkable only for David James setting a Premiership record for clean sheets, and unfortunately for Rupert Murdoch the whole sorry 90 minutes is broadcast on his channel, billed as *Super Sunday*. Even Andy Gray would have difficulty sounding excited about this and although I've set the TV at home to record, I certainly won't be sitting through it again. There was a flurry of excitement seeming to come from the Holte as stewards moved in to eject a couple of what I presume were its more volatile inhabitants but luckily it was all over quickly and the crowd could settle back to their Sunday afternoon snooze.

James earns his place in the record books with some good saves from Gardner, Gabby and Carew, but Pompey's 4-6-0 formation is hardly a recipe for thrilling entertainment, which perhaps explains the pitiful following they've brought with them from the south coast. Sadly, reports indicate that it includes That Twat With The Bell, so we all know who Sky will be focusing on. A couple of years ago when we were playing Portsmouth on TV, That Twat With The Bell was walking along Witton Lane posing for photos and doing all sorts of twattishness when a camera crew came sprinting up the road to film him as part of the 'authentic matchday atmosphere.' They totally ignored European Cup winners Gary Shaw and Tony Morley as they walked past.

Dave and I spend most of the ninety minutes discussing influential bands of the sixties. He's defending the honour of the Kinks, while I'm backing the Who. Neither of us consider the lovable moptops. Rich, much younger than both of us, listens in awe, not realising there was once a time when music was more than a collection of bleeps, thumps and bangs. You can't tell the boys from the girls these days either.

The end of the match signaled a move to eleventh in the table, even though it did also indicate just four points from our last five home games. Fortress Villa Park it ain't, but in truth it hasn't been for years. There's been a lot of debate, particularly in recent months on the internet, about whether we make it too easy for away teams by letting them have what I still call the Witton End even if North Stand Lower sounds better. I don't know about that – professional footballers shouldn't even notice who's sitting behind the goal – but it's been a long while since we had a team who'd battle for every blade of grass. Too many teams play us knowing they're going to get something even if they're not on top form.

Many more games like this and Wolfie and the rest of this season's born-again Villa fans won't be rushing back.

28th April
Manchester City (away)

The close-season's coming like a jail on wheels so to make the most of what's left of the fixture list me, Dave and Rich head up to Greater Manchester in Rich's works transport. We pass Doug on the way, being chauffered to another game. We wave but he ignores or, more likely, doesn't see us. There was a time when the very sight of him would have had me launching kamikaze lunges in an attempt to crash through the window of his Bentley, but I've mellowed now. He's not in control anymore, but fair play to him, he still goes to all the matches.

Also on the M6 are plenty of West Ham supporters on their way to Wigan. They already got the result of the season yesterday when they were fined £5.5 million over the Tevez and Mescherano affair but escaped a points deduction, so suddenly there's a glimmer of hope for them.

There's no sign of a decent pub near the ground nor anywhere to park that doesn't cost so it's into the official car park and our intrepid party split up. The other two knock out some quality literature while I have a mooch around what's an impressive-looking exterior then take my seat next to the home section, which as ever starts filling up with middle-aged Liam Gallagher wannabes and their unfortunate offspring. City's another place where a friendly reputation hides what can be a nasty place to visit. Maine Road could be a deathtrap for away supporters caught up in the maze of side streets and back alleys that surrounded the ground.

City start badly and get worse and we take the lead when Ashley Young, now beginning to justify his transfer fee, turns his marker inside out and sends over a perfect cross for Carew to head home.

As half time approaches Sorensen gives away a needless penalty but Barton slams the ball into the four thousand relieved Villa fans behind the goal, and about fifteen minutes from the end Shaun Maloney seals our third away win in a row with a sublime free kick. Not bad for someone who looks like he should be coming down the tunnel holding hands with the captain, shake hands with the ref and have his photo taken, then run off to his mom and dad.

It's no fluke that our improved form of late has coincided with the return of Craig Gardner and he puts in a characteristically whole-hearted display. His drive and tenacity are any manager's dream and his tackling so ferocious that I'd want shin-pads on just to interview him. His emergence has pushed crowd favourite Steven Davis down the pecking order and last season's player of the year is not even in the sixteen on duty today. If he wants to fulfill his undoubted potential he'll have to focus on his football, as playing Chesney in Corrie five times a week is not doing him any favours.

On the way back we stop off in Penkridge, a small town north of Wolverhampton and about half an hour from home. Our mood is slightly dampened by the fact that Blues got a late winner against Sheffield Wednesday, therefore just about guaranteeing them promotion. We were drinking away happily when some bloke who'd overheard us on about the match said, *"You Villa then? We'em gonna batter you again next season."*

"Really?" I said, and returned to our previous discussion about existentialist relativity, or it might have been the weather forecast. Both are equally unintelligible to an eavesdropping lower order.

"Ar," came the reply. *"Be nice to have a proper Brummie club in the Premiership. Least our fans am all from Birmingham."*

We'd clocked his hybrid Black Country/rural accent but it was Rich who got there first. *"Which part of Birmingham you from then?"*

"I aye from Brum. I live just down the road 'ere."

Living on Chelmsley has taught me many things, not least not to take the piss out of anyone in their own local when you're thirty miles from home, so the moment passed. His two mates had moved away, out of shame I would hope. We drank up, wished the Brummie farmhand a pleasant evening and didn't burst out laughing until we were safely out of stoning distance.

30th April

Derby lost yesterday, which meant automatic promotion to the Premiership for Birmingham City Football Club, or whatever they're called these days. They change their name so often I've stopped trying to keep up. *Midlands Today* had a camera crew at their ground, and in between the scenes of urban dereliction they managed to find a group of badly-clothed urchins to film celebrating this achievement. The immediate reaction of the first one they spoke to was, *"Bring on the Villa."* I don't have to add another word.

Chapter 11

Proud history, bright future

5th May

Sheffield United (home)

As always for the final home game, it's a sunny day. The last *H&V* of the season sells out early, to howls of anguish from Dave, who spends the rest of the day moaning that he should have had extra copies printed. Sadly, though, not early enough for me to witness the heroes of '82 parade the European Cup before the game. While that's happening I'm on the way into the ground when I spy a historic meeting between two retired veterans of the old days, one of them now a respected hoolie-author and the other a bit older and dressed in an unseasonable raincoat. Just to add to the atmosphere, a brief scuffle kicks off between some Sheffield United lads walking down from the Witton Arms (as we should really call it given the nature of the day) and a group of young ne'erdowells who suddenly appear from the North Stand car park. It looks like something serious might develop but the police are quickly in between both groups, draw their batons to get the Sheffield contingent out of harm's way and then push the home team back from whence they came. In the old days there'd have been a few arrests but now the police are content to stick cameras in the ringleaders' faces. That's progress for you.

By the time I get to my seat the '82 team have disappeared back down the tunnel and it's the turn of the current side to be lauded by the capacity crowd. The free scarves provided by the club, bearing the legend/marketing slogan of *"Proud History,*

Bright Future", are used to good effect in whipping up the atmosphere, and the fancy dress party among the Sheffield United fans adds to the celebratory mood.

Villa's play is brilliant as the bright sunshine as we crush the opposition thanks to quality goals from Gabby, Young (another who's come through a rough patch to look the part now) and Berger with a midfield masterclass from Gareth Barry. Sheffield United are woeful, head and shoulders the worst team we've played all season, but they're staying up barring a calamitous series of results so they've obviously decided to start their holidays early.

Looking round the team you can see something's finally coming together. It's the same rush of pride I had when my children took their first steps. It might not seem much to the casual observer but you just know there's going to be so much more where that came from. Gabby Agbonlahor, for instance. We've seen plenty of players who promised much but delivered a lot less. Yet you know Gabby's going to be a big start. He's got the attributes of a natural footballer but also the attitude of the top ones. I don't think I've seen him fazed wherever he's played. There was that patch a few weeks ago when he looked like he should be dropped but he came through that and I'd have him in the England squad right now. I'd also have Gareth Barry in there, as would anyone else in their right mind, but there's no point going on about that particular injustice.

The only blot on the landscape is provided by West Midlands Police who, in keeping with the nostalgic flavour of the afternoon, remind us of the time when they were feared the length and breadth of the land by treating a conga in the away end like a threat to national security. It's nice that we can all sleep safely in our beds knowing Fred Flinstone, Barney Rubble and Scooby-Doo are behind bars.

This time last year we were treated to a lap of dishonour, when David O'Leary hid behind the players and their kids to avoid the well-deserved stick he would otherwise have taken, not that it stopped at least four of us from hurling assorted oaths as he walked past. What a contrast to this day of remembering the past and looking forward full of hope for the future. In the last twelve months we've seen improvements on the pitch and some dazzling public relations – today's the day when it all comes together. The players and their children walk round the pitch in the warm evening air, basking in the adulation. The WAGs stay in the players tunnel (there's a joke in there but I'm too pure of thought to explore the possibilities) taking photos and exuding the confidence that comes from being stinking rich and impossibly thin.

7th May

Sir Graham Taylor once said, *"Finishing second is nothing to celebrate."* Not if you've got class it isn't. Otherwise it's worth a full civic reception. I read the *Mail* pullout, watch the news, listen to the news, see the multitudes piling off the bus from town and begin to wonder, not for the first time, if maybe they're right, and it's the rest of the world that's wrong. The answer to such sociological imponderables can only be found at the bottom of a glass so I head off to the White Hart, looking for inspiration. Pushing the door open I see what can only be described as a Styxian vision. Artists would describe such a scene as post-Apocalyptic. I'd call it 'Small Heath celebrates.' And go home, quickly.

13th May
Bolton Wanderers (away)

To a traditionalist like me, Bolton at the Reebok is 21st Century football hell. As well as the sulking Anelka and the snarling, diving and spitting of El Hadj-Diouff, the rest of the team is populated by the kind of mercenaries you'd expect when the recently departed manager had such allegedly cosy relationships with the vile parasites known as players agents. Like those agents, Bolton's football is all about percentages mixed with a bit of brute force and the stadium is so lacking in 'soul' they resort to playing James Brown when they score to get the crowd going. Allardyce went a few days ago, amidst rumours that he wanted to escape before the bungs enquiry got a bit too close to home, and Little Sammy Lee is in charge.

In spite of all that, it's my last chance to see this exciting, embryonic Villa side for three months and after last Saturday I don't want to miss a thing. Many of the claret and blue army are going in fancy dress, and most of them seem to have dressed as pirates. I enter the spirit of things by dressing up as an aging mod.

Rich does the driving again. Heavy traffic on the motorway, much of it West Ham going to up Old Trafford hoping to seal an escape that looked impossible a month ago and is now merely difficult, scuppers our chance of pre-match drinking and the only parking spot is a grass verge half a mile away. Painful experience has told us that under no circumstances do you park in the Reebok's officially-designated spots. Even I know that, and I don't drive. Luckily our pilot used to work these parts of the frozen north, so he knows the best places to hide a van from traffic wardens.

Inside the ground our young 'uns are in fine voice. They might be a pain sometimes but they know how to get behind the team. We go behind twice to typically scrappy Bolton goals, only to equalise both times with stunning finishes from Gardner and Moore and the noise doesn't stop. If nothing else, this season has shown what a bit of optimism can do to the supporters who were turning up last year more out of routine than anything else. All we need to do is channel that optimism into something a bit more concrete and the crowds will flood back. That's what a bit of sunshine and two equalisers does for you. At the end it's Bolton who are hanging on for the point they need to qualify for Europe. I can't help feeling that next season it'll be us in that position.

Elsewhere the last day of the season is throwing up a surprise as West Ham get three points at Old Trafford, with Carlos Tevez naturally scoring, and Wigan winning at Bramall Lane. So Neil Warnock's going down, and for all his outrage you can't but help feel some sympathy. As David O'Leary found out last season, if you claim the world's against you, don't be surprised when it starts to be. But while I don't think there's a conspiracy to send his team back form whence they came, I do agree that if Wigan or Sheffield United had been up before the beak, they'd have had points deducted. The Premier League doesn't want its television schedules clogged with clubs from grim northern towns playing grim northern football.

We drive away from the ground in reflective mood. The last match of the season is always a time for reflection. This time last year we couldn't celebrate Small Heath going down because we knew we'd be following them in twelve months time. What a difference a year makes.

We finish eleventh with fifty points and although at a glance that looks like an average season, if you've followed the Villa for a few years you'll know we don't do average. We replaced a regime that was out of touch, out of ideas and out of money with a dynamic new board led by a 44-year-old billionaire.

In place of a manager who's won nothing and didn't give a damn about the Villa, we employed a successful coach with an infectious passion for the club. Our formerly run-down training ground now has facilities that rank amongst the best in the world.

The once-crumbling Holte Hotel will soon be a striking landmark, as much a symbol of Randy Lerner's Villa as the decay and dereliction of the place in the last days of the previous regime. Like Aston Villa, it's got a new lease of life.

And I've changed from a miseryarsed malcontent, attending protest meetings and boycotting matches (though never being able to stay away completely), to a smiling scarf-twirler. I sold my shares but became part of the club again, and when the Villa family gets its focus like that there's no stopping us.

Postscript

14th June

I wanted to end this story on a positive note, but a few days after the season ended I learned of the death of Dave Nolan, killed in a freak accident while on holiday in Thailand. Details were sketchy but it appears he slipped in the bathroom, severed an artery and bled to death in hospital.

Known on the Birmingham club scene as Dave the Rave, his finely-honed diplomatic skills once made him the best doorman in town. Seriously, he never had to resort to violence; I honestly don't know if he was any good at it. I never saw him have an argument, let alone a fight. He was one bloke you were always glad to see and he had the ability to let you know the feeling was mutual. He brought up his kids, who were a credit to him, in the claret and blue tradition, aided by the odd complimentary fanzine from yours truly.

Dave had hundreds of mates around the city, and we gathered for his funeral at Olton Friary to celebrate a wonderful life rather than mourn a premature death. I for one will never forget him.

Also available from Heroes Publishing

AFTER THE VILLA
life without the lions
by DAVE WOODHALL

In the days before footballers retired as multi-millionaires,
they usually had to get a proper job once their
playing days were over.
After The Villa is the story of what happened to former
idols once they left Villa Park.
Peter McParland tells of his brush with a military dictator.
John Gidman describes how he fell foul of Special Branch.
Shaun Teale outlines the pain and glory of a non-league boss.
And a World Cup star claims he "wasn't much cop".
Essential reading for anyone who wonders just where it is
that old footballers go when they hang up their boots.

Price – £9.95
ISBN – 0954388437

Also available from Heroes Publishing

HUNDRED WATTS
a life in music
by RON WATTS

With Foreword by former Sex Pistol
Glen Matlock

Ron Watts remains one of the most influential men in
the history of British music.
From John Lee Hooker to Johnny Rotten, Bowie to Bono,
Ron got to know and work with the biggest and the best.
From bringing Blues greats to Britain, to his central role
in the 1976 Punk Festival at London's legendary 100 Club,
he helped shape youth culture in the UK.
Hundred Watts is the informative, revealing and extremely
funny account of his days at the cutting edge
of the music business.
Price – £7.99
ISBN – 0954388445

Also available from Heroes Publishing

HERBERT CHAPMAN
the first great manager
by SIMON PAGE

The son of a bare-knuckle fighting coal miner, Herbert
Chapman became the most famous football manager of his day.
One of the game's true immortals, he took Northampton Town,
Leeds City, Huddersfield Town and Arsenal to heights few had
ever dreamed possible. Yet his career nearly ended when he
was handed a lifetime ban in one of the game's earliest, biggest
and most notorious "bungs" scandals.
Including never before published family photographs and
stories, this book looks at the life of the man who stands at the
head of the list of English football's foremost bosses; the
forerunner of Busby, Shankly, Paisley, Clough and Ferguson –
the first great manager.

Price – £9.95
ISBN 0954388453 – EAN 9780954388454

HEROES PUBLISHING
PO Box 1703, Perry Barr, Birmingham, B42 1UZ
www.heroespublishing.com